SET FREE

A Woman's Guide to Clarity, Freedom, and God's Endless Love

JILL ALLEN

WESTBOW
P R E S S®
A DIVISION OF THOMAS NELSON
& ZONDERVAN

WestBow Press books may be ordered through booksellers or by contacting:

WestBow Press
A Division of Thomas Nelson & Zondervan
1663 Liberty Drive
Bloomington, IN 47403
www.westbowpress.com
844-714-3454

Scripture quotations taken from The Holy Bible, New International Version® NIV® Copyright © 1973 1978 1984 2011 by Biblica, Inc. TM. Used by permission. All rights reserved worldwide.

ISBN: 978-1-6642-2685-2 (sc)
ISBN: 978-1-6642-2686-9 (hc)
ISBN: 978-1-6642-2684-5 (e)

Library of Congress Control Number: 2021904861

Printed in the United States.

WestBow Press rev. date: 4/27/2021

To my Lord and Savior;
my husband, Rob;
my sons, Houston, Harrison, and Hayden;
and my daughters, Harper and Hadley

CONTENTS

INTRODUCTION

Have you ever felt like something was missing either within yourself or in your life? Like you just can't seem to put your finger on it, but you know there's a void ... somewhere. You wake up every day just to go through the motions, yet deep inside you crave more, and you know this is no way to truly live.

Maybe you've felt like you're living in the middle of a powerful, raging storm. Wherever you go, there's a dark cloud of rain following your every step. Perhaps your thoughts have drifted off, and you've found yourself questioning the meaning of life, and maybe you've thought, *There has to be more to life than this.*

You've been trying to find your purpose, and sometimes you even question whether you have one. You're left with this undeniable, unsettling pit in your stomach, and ultimately you just feel lost and alone.

You've asked yourself questions and whispered to heaven,

"What am I here to do, God?"

"Who am I supposed to be?"

"Do I have what it takes?"

"Where do I start?"

So far, this journey has led you to feelings of loneliness, sadness, anger, resentment, frustration, bitterness, fearfulness, and anxiety.

You name it—I have felt it all, too.

I get it, girlfriend.

Here's the truth. You are not showing up as the woman you desire to be, let alone who God designed and created you to be.

The world has shaped our vision of how life should be. It has painted the picture that experiencing crazy chaos, striving for more, and maintaining a busy life are somehow the perfect depiction of fulfillment and success. Somewhere along the way, we find ourselves chasing things that in the end ultimately don't matter.

We often try to convince ourselves that "this is how life works." In the process, we subconsciously enter the rat race, but all the while, we're suffering in silence, feeling empty, stressed to the brim. And before we realize it, life just passes us by. We forget we have a calling on our lives, and the world's vision is so polar opposite from the calling God has placed on us. "'For I know the plans I have for you,' declares the Lord, 'plans to prosper you and not to harm you, plans to give you hope and a future'" (Jeremiah 29:11 NIV).

Let me tell you—if life didn't have us on a speeding, twisting roller-coaster ride, taking us through difficult challenges and up and down the steep mountains, we would never discover who God intended us to be. I can honestly say that every heartache, setback, trial, and challenge I have had helped make me the strong, fierce woman I am today. Everything—the good, the bad, and the ugly—has helped mold me for a divine purpose and put me on a path that continually allows me to step into my greatness and my God-given purpose.

This is all part of a bigger, more intrinsic plan I so wish I could see (thanks to my type A personality), but the gift hidden within not knowing is learning to trust. The journey God has me on is one in which I am learning to fully trust.

I was in my closet, hiding from my five incredible, wild, yet crazy children, when I turned on some worship music to spiritually recharge. Now, if you had asked me just one year ago whether I would be going to God first with everything, I probably would have just nodded and smiled politely.

Maybe you can relate, but I have always been one to take control and do it all by myself. Looking back, I can say I even thrived on that plan. So taking the time to be still and to listen to what God was telling me might have been a *slight* challenge. However, when I slow down just enough to truly listen for my next steps, I have learned that this method is good for my soul and all those around me. I encourage you to try it.

> He says, "Be still, and know that I am God;
> I will be exalted among the nations,
> I will be exalted in the earth."
> (Psalm 46:10 NIV)

As I was taking it all in, I could hear, "Your God-given story is your message."

The words were spoken to me loud and clear; like a mantra (or a broken record), they kept repeating and wouldn't go away.

It was like the music softened, and they were coming out of the speaker on repeat, playing over and over again in my heart and mind.

Now here we are, just a few short weeks later, and I'm typing away as if I were born to do this—even though I was the one who failed my twelfth-grade state writing proficiency test. Here I am, sharing my story with you.

This book is my gift to you. I hope it helps to restore your faith with encouragement so you can turn your struggles into fuel, which inspires you to shine your light ever so brightly and transforms you into the woman you have always been called to be.

There will be a time when you recall that precious moment when you took a deep dive into your heart and were willing to say "Yes!" to all the blessings and gifts God has given you. And with that "Yes!" will also be the first step on your journey, which is aligned with your purpose.

Let's begin.

CHAPTER 1
THE CALLING FOR GREATNESS

Before I formed you in the womb I knew you,
before you were born I set you apart;
I appointed you as a prophet to the nations.

—Jeremiah 1:5 (NIV)

Wham. What happened? I think my husband, Rob, just ran over my eighteen-week-pregnant self with his Ford F-350, a three-fourth-ton diesel snowplow. I got knocked down, run over, and watched in shock as the drive shaft spun over me.

Talk about your life flashing before your eyes.

In his defense, my husband had no idea what had just happened. I was behind his truck, shoveling snow off the sidewalk. He couldn't see me.

Let me start from the beginning. It was a cold winter day in February, and I was home with my three boys, who were all under four years old. The snow had piled up outside, and that meant Rob would have had to plow for days. It was just that time of year. But it was a typical day for me—my toddlers were running around, and I was cooped up in the house with raging hormones, desperate to get outside and do something.

I remember calling Rob and begging him to pick us up so we could help him. Looking back, I recall we weren't much help. He reluctantly said he would swing by to pick us up and that I could shovel the sidewalks if I wanted to. I made snack bags for the boys and bundled all of them up with their sippy cups.

The rumbling truck headed up the driveway, and we waved him down because we were so excited to leave the house. Our first job was a success. I remember hopping back into the truck, thanking him for picking us up, and feeling grateful for the fresh air we all needed. I remember the boys grinning in their car seats, chowing down on animal crackers; they didn't have a care in the world.

At the next house, a miracle happened.

I jumped out of the truck and grabbed a shovel; it was go time. I headed over to where the sidewalk met the driveway. I looked over, and Rob was parked and on his phone. His phone rang nonstop with everyone who wanted to be first on the list.

I bent down to get my legs into that initial shove, and then he threw the truck in reverse. The truck collided with my left hip and threw me about five feet. He kept going. The back tires ran over my left shoulder and my head as I stared up at the truck, bewildered.

I knew the front tires were coming my way next and then the plow.

But then the truck stopped. For a split second, I thought I was safe. Then the shifting sounds began.

I knew Rob didn't know what was happening. He shifted the truck back into drive (he later told me he thought he had hit a mulch bed). He was going to pull forward. My mind was racing, and I felt like my adrenaline was in overdrive. By God's grace, I scrambled out from under the truck with my broken shovel in hand. I waved my arms, covered in snow, and screamed to get Rob's attention. He stopped and rolled down the window.

He asked me why I was making snow angels, completely unaware that I had just been under his truck. Now, crying uncontrollably, I barely uttered, "You just ran over me."

He jumped out of the truck and ran toward me, speechless.

I felt fine. I thought I was okay. All I could think about was the baby girl I was carrying. We rushed to the hospital. Except for some hair loss from the rubber tire, a few bruises, and feeling a little shaken up—oh, and my new Victoria's Secret bra had gotten torn up—I walked away relatively unscathed.

The baby was perfectly fine. Our little Harper Lyn was safe. There was no need for an explanation. The entire event didn't make any sense.

The nurses at the ER asked how I was doing. Their jaws dropped to the ground when I explained what had happened.

In the days that followed, we joked about how we always knew I had a hard head, and this event just proved it. But honestly, we knew it was a gift from up above that I had survived—a miracle. We knew my time on earth wasn't finished and that I was here for a reason. As are you!

We often get distracted from our true callings and go through life living in a fog. I don't think we all need to be hit by a truck to realize fundamental truths. However, we do need to wake up and realize our real purposes.

Something shifted within me in a significant way. I knew this, I talked about it, but I'm not sure whether I actively lived it. The meaning of my life wasn't about my successes, accomplishments, or dreams. I wanted to live a life of meaning.

Still, I followed the wrong things. On the flip side, I also think we totally miss all of God's goodness and the call He has on our life because we live in an aimless fog.

Living in a Fog

Do you hit the snooze button every morning? Not because you're tired but because you're not fired up about your day? How about Sundays? Do you dread those Mondays?

I cannot tell you how many people I talk to who just try to get through the day, however they can. You might be like me. Do you have everything the world values yet still hunger for more? Maybe you can't quite put your finger on what this hunger is. It fascinates me when I hear people talk about their lives and their passions with such conviction, but it saddens me when people feel like something is missing from their lives.

Do you have that spark that drives you? Do you have passion, a purpose, a mission, or a dream that inspires you and gets you out of bed before your alarm clock because your mind is racing with ideas? Do you feel alive, or are you going through life while living in a fog? That's what we'll talk about.

I'm going to teach you how to start living your life with purpose by finding your passion. And this topic excites me.

So the question is, how?

Step one: wake up.

Are you trapped in the cycle of daily being too busy and just waiting for the weekend to finally arrive? Does life feel like it's passing you by? Are you going through the motions, just settling, and living a life of mediocrity?

It's time for a much-needed wake-up call, friend.

If you don't have any new goals or dreams you want to pursue, there is nothing to reach for. You are operating on autopilot. You live in a fog, and something is missing. You can't live your best life. So if you're in a funk, let's be direct. Stop lying to yourself; no more fooling around. Take a long pause to truly reflect, ground yourself with a clear perspective, and ask yourself where you are.

What's going on that's good? What do you have to be grateful for? Are you truly happy? What are you passionate about? What's holding you back from pursuing it?

These are the questions to ask regarding the whole trajectory of your life.

I won't waste another minute stuck in a comfortable routine. Living in a fog just doesn't work for me anymore. So now's the time for serious self-reflection. It's a decision you can make for yourself to be fully conscious and self-aware in real time.

Step two: find your passion.

Deep down you know what you are passionate about. You have a dream and a mission. But too often our passions and dreams can get buried by the demands of everyday life. So the question is, how do you find your passion? Where do you even begin? Okay, so I have a few things I want to share with you. I want you to try something new.

Do something that scares you. Maybe take a fitness class or cooking class, go on a retreat, or take a trip to an exotic place. Just do something different. If you try a few things that scare you, which you never figured you would try, something will resonate, and an alarm will go off in your heart. You'll be in your element. You'll instinctively become aware of what you're passionate about. But I want you to be mindful of distractions and errors in judgment. Search for something more meaningful. I'm here to encourage you to fight through the fog and hone in on what inspires you. Ask yourself what brings you true bliss.

Now, this step often feels effortless for me. Helping women reach breakthroughs, chase their dreams with wild abandon, and live their lives with inspiration is what fires me up.

What fires you up? What lights you up and makes you lose track of time? I love hiking. I feel in my element. The key is to give myself *permission* to enjoy doing what I love and the *conviction* to know I deserve it.

It's impossible to reach your potential if you don't take the time to discover it. So we've got to stick to the process, stick with this journey, and fight for it. But first, we need to understand that it is a journey. I want you to attack this journey head-on to discover how you can actually contribute to the world in your unique way.

What makes you feel useful, inspired, and alive?

Think about what brings you true happiness and a sense of self-worth. It's always a sense of purpose and never material things. Beauty, money, and career success are superficial distractions. Our mission in life is to find meaning and purpose, not to pursue the appearance of success defined by our culture's expectations. And this mission won't fall into our laps—we need to seek it out.

It's about discovering the thing that makes you tick and committing your life to it.

Think about that.

Let me repeat. It's about discovering the thing that makes you tick and then committing your life to it.

So search for it, figure it out, chase it down, or stumble upon it by sheer luck. And when you do, your passion will shine brightly through you and navigate your life.

Your infection of love and purpose will be contagious.

Next, figure out what you want.

What do you dream about? What is it you really want out of life?

Okay, you're starting to wake up, taking that first step toward finding your passion, but you first need to ask yourself, *What is it I really want out of life?* When you discover your passion, you will probably unearth something that has been brewing inside you for a long time that you simply needed to pay attention to. You've broken through the fog. You've finally realized you need to live your life with passion. Sadly, most of us never come to that realization.

Let's take the time to ask ourselves this question.

So let me ask you again. What is it that you really want?

Remember, this is your life, your dreams, and your most incredible adventure. You owe it to God and His people to discover what your real purpose is. Think about the impact your next move will have on the world.

What defines you?

What will you not tolerate in your life, and what will you accept?

What do you value?

Take time to examine your life and discover what you really want. The majority of us are living on autopilot. But here's the thing. You can take control of your thoughts, feelings, and destiny.

I get it.

After we graduate from high school, we learn the mainstream ideology of what life should be—go to college, pursue a career, have a family, and buy a house. Society teaches us to "take it all on" and that being busy is somehow successful. Then we end up on the soul-searching journey like most people we encounter in life.

But the truth is that both our failures and successes are all part of God's divine plan for our lives. We have two choices in life. We can hand the controls back to God, trust Him, and answer our calling. Or we can try to be our own superhero and take on the weight of the world and the burdens it carries.

Thanks to Carrie Underwood, we can all hear the song ringing in our ears for "Jesus, Take the Wheel." And we know that ultimately God is in control of our lives. We have control over how much we choose to carry and how much of it we give to Him. We have free will, which allows us to walk toward God or run away, to take a step forward or backward, to listen to Him or not. Life can be whatever we choose, and I don't want you to sell yourself short by ignoring what your passion truly is and not sharing your dreams. You are so much more valuable to the world and everyone around you when you live with passion and purpose.

I hope I've lifted the fog to inspire you to take action to do something different—to answer the call of your soul to live life with intention and purpose.

Wake-Up Call Moments

I believe we are all here for a reason. I know God put us here to fulfill a purpose that enriches us and gives Him joy. Over the past few years, I've been intentionally seeking Him to find my purpose to live a more fulfilled life. We naturally question it when we are called on this journey, and we often feel inadequate. "Wait, me? You want me to aim for that?" We will be called to exceed our expectations and to have the courage to face our real purpose.

Have you been trying to find your calling? Or maybe you just feel like something is missing in your life; you are feeling content perhaps but unfulfilled. I've been there, and on some days I still feel that way. I've learned how important it is to live life with *intention*, because living life passively isn't really living. You can't just keep floating through life. Trust me. I've definitely figured that out by now.

It was difficult for me to balance doing what society expected me to do and doing what God wanted me to do. We have to make a living, provide for our families, and do so much more. But we still need to find a way to do all that without getting caught up in things that hijack our sense of peace and connection to God.

I had to recognize God's calling for myself. It often comes as a gentle nudge, a whisper, or a loud bang we choose to ignore. You need to learn to recognize it when it comes. How many more signs do we really need?

I know how difficult it can be to feel like you're just moving through life without a real direction. I have discovered how important it is to identify your calling in life. If you've been dealing with this issue, just take a moment to answer these questions.

What does your most fulfilling life look like?

What is God calling you to do? Are you being obedient? Why or why not?

How much time do you spend in the Word – worshipping, praying, reading the Bible, in sisterhood, church, and so on?

How can you grow closer to God?

What brings you real joy?

What could you do more of to live a life of pure joy?

What mission has the Lord revealed to you?

How are you using the gift of your life?

I want you to be able to move past this challenge. I want you to experience joy and fulfillment in your life and to follow God's calling for you.

Now that you've realized you may not be living your life to the fullest, here's what you can do to change that.

It's time to find what brings you joy and makes you feel fulfilled. Think about all the things you do on a weekly or daily basis. What makes you the happiest? Once you figure that out, I want you to focus on one specific thing every day to fine-tune your everyday life's direction and clarity.

I want you to take this verse with you today and reflect on it as you think about your true calling:

"Each of you should use whatever gift you have received to serve others, as faithful stewards of God's grace in its various forms" (1 Peter 4:10 NIV).

CHAPTER 2
CHIPPING AWAY AT OUR IDENTITY

For we are God's handiwork, created in Christ Jesus to do
good works, which God prepared in advance for us to do.

—Ephesians 2:10 (NIV)

I am cruising through life. I am a wife and have been married for almost
twenty-one years to the love of my life, Rob. I am a proud mom of
five amazing, crazy kids. I am also blessed to have a career that fulfills
my passion and purpose. Coaching women to be their best selves—it
doesn't get any better than that.

I am the doer, the performer, the one who loves to excel, the overachiever,
the one who is always in control, the one who can get it done. I give my
best every day; that is me. And now that I have painted that picture-
perfect life for you, allow me to be open and vulnerable for a moment
about something I often struggle with.

I really like the perfect version of me more. At least I thought so.

Before you hit forty and face your first midlife crisis, you don't know
who you were meant to be, even though you've probably experimented
and struggled to find your life's path. At that stage of life, you barely
have time to gauge who you really are and what your role is ... the wife,
mom, career-driven woman, business owner, coach, leader, friend,

sister, aunt, daughter, Uber driver. You name it. We all play those roles very well. I'm sure you can relate.

Have you ever asked yourself, *Who am I?* No joking here, ladies. I know I am not the only one who has tried to figure it all out. I lost myself— not physically but in the sense that I felt like I was spinning my wheels, questioning my purpose and direction, and trying to figure out who I really was. I felt tired of trying to keep up with the perfect image and just wanted the "real Jill" to show up. I wanted the "fun Jill" to show up. Fun meant the easygoing, laid-back Jill. If there even was a "fun Jill," where was she, and why had I ignored her for so long? But is that who I was at my core? Did a "fun Jill" even exist?

I tried to think back to when I was a little girl. I remember playing with Barbies with my friend Jenny, enjoying kickball in the street and hide-and-seek with the neighborhood kids, riding bikes in the middle of the road until the streetlights kicked on, putting on our "creek" shoes and wading in the stream, catching crawdads and minnows all day, throwing them in a bucket and letting them go at the end of the day. I was a totally carefree kid.

I was the kid who would pee her pants from laughing so hard. Where did that girl go? I asked my grandma what I was like when I was little, and she said I took the book from my preschool teacher and read to the class myself ... even turning the book around to show everyone the pictures. So I might have shown some leadership skills and go-getter traits early on. That's just my personality.

I vividly remember one day I hadn't spoken about for thirty-four years that changed everything. Eek. I told you I was going to be open and vulnerable.

I was nine years old and in the fourth grade. My principal came in to grab me from the classroom. How cool. I thought I was being excused in the middle of class. I got up with a smile, grinned at my classmates, and headed toward the door. He told me to grab my book bag. He escorted me to the small band room.

My seven-year-old brother walked toward me, and we went in together. Our two aunts greeted us with hugs; the two women had to tell a nine- and seven-year-old that their mother had been killed in a car accident that morning. That day the course of our lives changed forever.

Crazy to think of those simpler times. We were hotshots that first day while riding our bikes to school. I thought, *Who would grab our bikes?* Mom had packed Lunchables for our lunch that day. Another first. A special treat. We didn't get to eat them. You remember those; they must have come out in the mid-1980s, and you were so cool to have those for lunch.

You wouldn't catch me buying one of those for my kids today. I know Lunchables aren't things you'd typically remember on the day your mom died, but it's crazy how the brain works amid tragedy. You sort of go into survival mode, focusing on the trivial things. I asked myself, *Did she have her seatbelt on?*

I tried to make sense of it all to preserve myself in the enormity of it all. My dad was on his annual Canada fishing trip in the middle of nowhere and a floatplane away before he'd reach civilization. It took a few days for him to finally get home. I just remember the three of us downstairs, sitting on my grandma and grandpa's basement couch. We sat there and cried. I remember my dad (all six four of him) wrapping his arms around us and telling us everything would be okay one day.

I changed that day, whether I knew it or not. Who wouldn't change? Who I thought I should be, who I was, how I looked at the world, my beliefs, thoughts, behaviors, and perspective of a family—everything changed. I grew up overnight. I had to. The kid in me left, and I felt the need to become an adult overnight.

Disclaimer: I have the best family ever and had a loving, wonderful childhood. I chose not to let this event define me. It just made me stronger and my purpose even greater. That's not to say it was easy; far from it. We all have stories, people, and events in our lives that help shape who we are, but we often don't even realize that until we grow up and reflect on the journey. Who do we think we need to be, and how do we show up in the world? What foundation have we created? What beliefs do we have about ourselves, and how do we create a false narrative about ourselves?

Think back to when you were a child. Did you have a picture-perfect childhood? Were you the honor student, the star athlete, the overachiever, the goal crusher? Did you do anything to meet expectations? Or did you grow up in a broken home, a child of abuse, drug addicts, or alcoholic parents? At the end of the day, your past doesn't define you. You have one identity that has already been given to you through Christ. There are no labels—simply one identity, one purpose, one character that is you. And there is only one *you*.

Who and what have shaped you into who you are today? Who spoke to your heart? What did the person tell you that changed you? What did you begin to believe about yourself or your perspective on life? When did you become focused on what others thought? When did you start comparing yourself to others? When did you begin to be a people pleaser? When did you start doing too much of the wrong thing? When did you seek attention? When did you crave recognition? When did you start conforming to the world's views, beliefs, and expectations?

When did your God-given gifts get lost, hidden, or buried? Are you using your gifts to the fullest? When did you lose the passion? Where is that carefree little girl? When did insecurity and self-doubt set in? When did the fear show up? When did the need to control everything in your life take over? When did you start believing the lies we have been told? Not thin enough, not good enough, not worthy enough? Your dreams are unrealistic. You are incapable. Have you been told to follow the course, the norm, the mainstream? You shouldn't take risks. You can't do it. What plan are you following? Your parents' plan, your plan, or God's plan for you?

We need to get rid of these lies, these false beliefs, and mental barriers that do not align with God's word. We will get into that a bit more as we move forward with this journey. Who are you, and what defines you? What is your identity? What is your purpose? So many struggle to answer these questions. I have often been guilty of basing my identity on what I do—my career, my roles, my relationships, and my past. I've defined myself by those pursuits. I know I limit myself when I do that. God has bigger plans for me.

The truth is that God intends for us to find our identity in Christ. Why did it take me so long to figure that out? I missed out on so much love and peace, but it isn't too late for me because it's never too late for any of us to start right now. We aren't too old or too young. Our identity is rooted in the fact that we are beloved children of God. I am the daughter of the Lord. He calls me just as He calls you. He calls upon us to remind us of who we truly are in Christ.

Who we think we are as individuals doesn't compare to who we truly are in Christ.

That fundamental cornerstone is where we should start to define ourselves.

God has "fearfully and wonderfully" made us as individuals with great, loving care. "I praise you because I am fearfully and wonderfully made; your works are wonderful, I know that full well" (Psalm 139:14 NIV).

So if He thought of us and created each of us with such intention, we need to understand His purpose for the lives He has given us.

I am a child of God—loved no matter what, loved for who I am. "Fear not, for I have redeemed you; I have summoned you by name; you are mine" (Isaiah 43:1 NIV).

The Lord knows our names. He calls them today. He calls us to show up as who He created us to be. Are we answering that call? Above all else, remember this: we are His, and we are not to get caught up in the roles we play in this life, nor the expectations, past, or false beliefs about who we are.

Our identity is in Christ, and that is all we need to know.

Wake-Up Call Moments

Who are you? Who are you meant to be?

I ask myself those questions a lot. I spent a lot of time in my life avoiding my true calling and lived how I thought I was supposed to live. I think about everything in my life that has led me to become who I am today. I'm sure you can think of specific events that have transformed you too.

It's so easy to let others and our cultural environment play a role in who we are. Someone might think you're not good enough to get that promotion. Someone might disagree with the life choices you've made. The list only goes on and on. Trust me, I've heard it all by now.

Plus, society has set expectations for what our values are and who we should be. You might feel the pressure to be a stay-at-home mom or a working mom. You might feel guilty about simply being a mom, like that isn't enough. You might feel something totally different. No matter what, I need you to step away from those feelings and pressures for a moment.

Why?

Because they're completely unimportant. I know it's easy to be distracted by everything we're expected to do. It's not hard to let others and our culture create our sense of identity. I've made this mistake plenty of times.

Fortunately, I've experienced some genuine growth in my life. I've figured out what my identity in Christ is. I have a hint for you. Not everyone is going to like your identity in Christ. There will be plenty of people who think you're on the wrong track.

You're not.

In truth, I'm focusing on my identity in God. We were all made with a purpose God has designed for us. When we get caught up with all the distractions and false beliefs happening in our lives, we don't live up to and honor our true identity.

If you're currently struggling to find your true purpose from God, it's important to reflect on those feelings. Work through these questions and dig deep. Listen to your heart. Pray and meditate on these questions to help you discover your true identity.

When you look in the mirror, whom do you see? Who do other people think you are? Who does God say you are?

Sometimes we mistake our identity for the one that has been given to us, the one we tell ourselves we should be. But this just holds us back and keeps us down, lamenting over who we wish we were rather than jumping for joy and embracing who we really are.

He gives us our identities and a mission, so we need to let go of our self-image, our dignity, and gain a sense of humility.

Talk about showing up as your most *authentic* self, right? Imagine how powerful that is.

Answer these questions to dive deeper into your identity:

What lies are you currently believing? Expose the lies.

How have these lies taken control and held you back from answering the call on your life?

Ask and sit down with the Lord, who do you say I am? Who am I Lord? Reveal the truth to me. Write your answers here.

Compare your identity in Christ to the identity you or others have set for you.

How will your identity in Christ change the atmosphere?

Invite Him into your heart. What truths is He speaking about who you are?

How does your new identity in Christ make you feel? How will understanding who you are in Christ change the way you show up in life?

Now I want you to focus on chipping away at your identity. This task might sound daunting. Remember that you should focus on your identity in Christ above all else.

You might think that a certain skill you have defines your identity. For example, if you're a skilled painter, you might believe that being an artist is your identity. I totally get where you are coming from. If you ever lost the ability to paint, you might feel like you lost your entire identity.

When we talk about our identity in Christ, we look for a concrete identity that doesn't fade. You might lose your talent, your ability to paint, but your identity in Christ will never diminish no matter what happens.

I have a verse I would love for you to reflect on as you try to discover your identity in Christ. Think about what this means for you and how it can help you walk away from the world's expectations and pressures. "And to put on the new self, created to be like God in true righteousness and holiness" (Ephesians 4:24 NIV).

CHAPTER 3
TIPTOEING AROUND

And without faith it is impossible to please God, because
anyone who comes to him must believe that he exists
and that he rewards those who earnestly seek him.

—Hebrews 11:6 (NIV)

To be honest, I was a yo-yo Christian. Is there even such a thing? I
know all about the yo-yo dieters and the up-and-down cycles when it
comes to fitness. That's the most common example of "yo-yoing," but
that's not how it happened with me.

This "yo-yo effect" had a serious impact on my faith. When it came
to my faith, I was never consistent. I was hot and cold, faithful when I
thought it would serve me, faithless when I thought it wouldn't. I was
gung ho, and then I was just lazy. I was brimming with so-called faith;
then I went down that dark rabbit hole of doubt. I asked myself, "Am
I good enough? Am I worth it?" I questioned everything, allowing
worry and fear to control my life. I opened the door to doubt, a feeling
I know you've felt.

This whole yo-yo cycle was a hard thing for me to go through as a
Christian. I wanted to be a "good" Christian, and I wanted to follow
God's plan for me. I just couldn't stick to it. I kept falling in and out of
my faith. I ended up doubting myself and God, a fact that pained me
even more. It was a heartbreaking experience, and I didn't know what

I was supposed to do. How was I supposed to fix this? I just felt utterly confused, frustrated, and afraid of everything. I felt lost.

I went through this constant cycle for most of my life. At times my faith was unshakable, and at others, it was weak or nonexistent. I didn't grow up in the church. As a matter of fact, I could probably count on one hand the number of times I attended a church service when I was young. In my junior high days, I joined a youth group with some friends, and I remember enjoying those nights when we got together. I loved the community and friendships. I had fun talking about the Lord and chowing down on snacks all night. I felt His presence there.

I feel like the youth group had a positive impact on my faith. It was an opportunity for me to connect with others my age who were struggling with the same things. We were all in the same boat, and we all cared about God and wanted to grow closer to Him. That was probably one of the highest points in my journey to regain my faith and become who I am today. It was a time when I felt truly passionate about God and His plan for me.

I reflect and question things often. I always see both sides of everything, but my flaw is that I have faith only when it is convenient. When everything goes smoothly as planned, it's easy to see God's love for me. Yet when I'm faced with a real challenge, my faith wavers, and I forget about the larger picture and what it means to truly have faith through difficult times. I wanted to be a better follower of Christ. I wanted to know with conviction that God was good, that He was always there through humble, unwavering belief.

I can only describe this experience with faith as baffling. I still held that lingering doubt that if I couldn't actually feel it, touch it, or see it, it wasn't real. Doubt always gnawed at me. The unwavering faith I thought I had would disappear. And with no mentor to guide me, I had persistent questions.

Unfortunately, I didn't give my faith a second thought throughout high school and college. I assumed it was a given and didn't consistently require work or self-reflection. I'm not sure what exactly happened at that point, but it just goes back to being a yo-yo believer for part of my life. I just kept going back and forth about religion, wondering where I fit in.

My best friend and college roommate, Darcey, loved to pray. I frankly thought she was nuts. She drove me crazy, always talking about the "good God above" and "Jesus who saves." Her emphasis just felt odd, and it was a lot for me to digest. It felt over the top. She was different. Jesus felt different, a foreign concept removed from who I was. Considering how I had grown up and how I lived my life then, Darcey's faith was just kind of weird to me. It was really just different from what was familiar. Religion was never a topic of discussion while growing up, so believing that having a relationship with Jesus was a game-changer was a bit much for me. But I know now that I was ignorant at that time. And because I wasn't really focused on my faith then, I wasn't sure what to think of it all. So I just continued to navigate life on my own.

Darcey and I were on completely opposite sides of the religious spectrum. She grew up with an intense church life. She was on fire for God. She was bold. You could even say she was radical. Putting the Lord first just wasn't my thing at the time. It got under my skin and drove me away. Her beliefs were against the norm and traditional, modern worldviews. Of course, it would drive someone away who already questioned his or her faith. I must have rolled my eyes at her constantly. She pushed me away, and I wanted nothing to do with her form of in-your-face, radical, unrelenting belief. My mind and heart were totally closed off to her. Persistent doubt made me reject her.

Looking back, I see that Darcey's constant praying and talking about God were all part of the plan. When I was in college, I didn't know how much impact my roommate would have on me. I strongly believe people are placed in your life for a reason. I think every person who comes into your life has some kind of purpose, whether that's positive, negative, or simply transformative. He or she might support or denigrate you, but the purpose is for you to learn an important lesson. The Lord was doing His work through Darcey as she planted the seeds. We need those people in our lives, people who plant those seeds of hope, love, and faith in our lives.

We need people who don't just say they will pray but actually do. No matter what was going on in her world, her faith and heart full of God's love for others always shined through. Because of her strength and faith, we are still best of friends today. Now when I think about Darcey, I think back to what an example she was and how her faith impacted more than just her. It impacted me. Even if I thought she was odd back then, I see now just how important that relationship was to my faith. And it still holds importance to this day. I am so thankful to have her in my life, since I know she has prayed wholeheartedly for me daily over the years.

When Rob and I got married, we decided to find a church community because we felt that was the next logical thing. I thought that was what we were supposed to do as a young married couple. So we searched for the perfect church for us, no questions asked. Once we found a church we liked, we started going weekly. That is just what you do as a young couple who are about to have their first child. We went to church every Sunday, just like we thought we should, and we enjoyed it. I felt God's presence, even in just the first hour we were there; it was an amazing feeling that made me feel so good. I felt like I was absorbing the word of God and that it was having a positive effect on my life.

And then we left and dove right back into our everyday, busy lives. Before long, we forgot or ignored or disregarded everything I had learned from the sermon. We weren't sure whether it would carry us through the week. It was all relegated to Sundays. Then during the rest of the week, I was busy and didn't pay much attention to God. We went back on Sundays, and the cycle of temporary pseudo faith started all over again.

Talk about the yo-yo cycle. I was the once-a-week Christian. I did everything right. I went to church. I taught Sunday school for a few years. Our kids went to a Christian preschool. I read daily devotions. Rob even gifted me with a beautiful Bible because I had said I would read the entire thing one year. I listened to worship music. I talked about my faith. I told people I would pray for them (and never took the time to actually do so). It was like I had this tug in my heart for years, even when I thought I was doing everything "right," but something was still missing.

I struggled with that for a little while. I didn't want something to be missing. I didn't want to keep feeling that way. I felt like I was putting all my effort into my faith and that I was doing enough. But I couldn't shake that feeling that something wasn't right or that something was missing. It took me a while to figure out the problem. I tried talking to Rob about it. I tried reading about it. I tried to find out what was missing, but I just wasn't getting anywhere.

Where was this inexplicable peace that faith promises? I strove for things that didn't fulfill me. My anxiety was at an all-time high, I was addicted to being busy, and I felt the need to control every minute of my day. I thought I was truly pursuing the Lord, but I wasn't grasping the concept fully. I don't think I really knew who or what the Lord truly was or what faith or devotion required. The connection was broken. I was given full access to God, but my heart never fully embraced that gift. And it wasn't like He was making it hard. I was the one overcomplicating it all with self-doubt.

Eventually, I figured out that I was just tiptoeing. Praying and spending time with the Lord were just part of my to-do list, but they weren't heartfelt or authentic. They were just more things I needed to do every day, like doing the dishes, working out, or going to the grocery store. I could check them off when completed for the day. I could then call myself a "good Christian" and sleep at night. At that point, prayer and faith were just as mundane as any other daily task; they had no real meaning. Say your prayers, read the Bible, do the dishes, lather, rinse, and repeat. I thought I was doing everything perfectly, yet I was still not truly living out His word, and I felt empty.

But eventually, I had a revelation. Doubt began to overshadow my life. I started to give in to doubt and fear. Bad things just happen sometimes, right? I chuckle now as I talk about this dark road of doubt because it's the kind of talk that would bring me back to the crazy days with my college roommate. That was back when I thought she was different or maybe just a little weird. Now I think, *You don't talk like that. You sound weird. You sound crazy.* Oh, how things can change! My faith has changed enormously since my high school and college days.

I eventually started to notice how doubt had permeated and influenced my entire life. Of course, I didn't realize it at the time. Again, I thought that bad things just happen sometimes. I felt that relationships just fell apart. My son moved out just two days after he turned eighteen. The magical number eighteen—you gotta love it.

I wish I could say it was his college move-in day, but I am being real with you here. It was more of the "When I turn eighteen, I am gone" move. Talk about a hard hit. If you have had a teenager, you can probably relate to what was going through my mind and how my heart ached that day. If not, I can't tell you how much it hurts—a lot. Our picture-perfect family was crumbling. Our relationship was strained.

I will spare you all the details but know that doubt and fear will jeopardize your most valued relationships. A moment like that can bring a mama to her knees. My son's move took me down a rabbit hole of questioning everything. *Am I a good mom? Did I do everything I could? What did I do wrong? Was I too harsh? Too strict? Not hard enough? How did I allow this to happen? It's my fault.*

There I was, beating myself up, crying uncontrollably, and repeating the endless cycle of doubting myself and my Lord and Savior.

This was such a hard time for me, not only as a mother but also as a believer. When I realized doubt and fear had something to do with it, I just wanted the situation to stop. I felt scared and confused, and I didn't know what I was supposed to do. It wasn't just a normal relationship falling apart. It was so much deeper than that.

When self-doubt and fear show up to divide, they show up as truth you need to face head-on in a mirror. They always feel real. They hit close to home and to what matters the most. And doubt and fear wear many faces to cause division and disruption. Doubt and fear don't necessarily show themselves with a pitchfork, horns, and a tail, guns blazing; they can be a subtle, pervasive, years-long infection of the soul. They strive to divide and conquer, tricking you into believing evil, hurt, and pain will control who you are and define your life. Self-doubt, fear, and insecurities will take us down if we give in to those emotions. It takes a special vigilance to recognize what they are to move forward with our life's purpose.

It's times like this when you have a choice. You might not feel like you have any say. You might feel like you're not strong enough to handle the battles you face. We can believe the lie and fight back in the flesh. I don't know about you, but I have been guilty of doing that, and it just isn't the person I want to be. Or we can walk boldly with our faith and show up with our hearts full of God's goodness. Easier said than done, I know.

I believed the lie that my son's moving out was all my fault. I believed the lie that he truly didn't like me. I believed I was a bad mother, that I was the reason our "perfect family" had fallen apart. I felt guilty and beaten. I blamed myself and wished I could do it all over again the right way. There had to be a reason. Don't even talk to me about spiritual warfare. It was easier to believe at face value what was happening to me, our family, and a relationship I craved with my son. It was easier to believe my distorted misperceptions about my reality than the eternal, uncompromising promise of God.

I can't believe I'm putting all this out there, but I know you need to hear this. We are in this together. I found myself caring more about what others would think when I shared my faith. I didn't want to sound crazy or put on that mask of perfection so many of us fall victim to. People are struggling daily. We just need genuine faith to persevere. We spend so much time just powering through, going through the routines, never really all in——but being lukewarm won't prepare us for the hard stuff life throws at us. So let's get real. Call it what it is. Commit. Devote yourself to Him. Actively seek Him.

Tiptoeing around is no longer an option. Going through the motions and doing things right don't cut it. Exposing the lies and deception isn't enough; it's about believing in God and His truth. It's about truly seeking Him and God's truth. But we can't decipher what the truth really is if we are lukewarm in our faith. Or we fall into the trap of fear and self-doubt because we assume subconsciously that our hearts and minds are totally separate from the Creator. We can have a passive belief in God while our hearts and minds are totally removed from our Creator. Having a relationship with Him triggers that aha moment when life is not just about knowing there is a god but connecting that belief to our hearts and minds, and fostering that close relationship and connection with Jesus.

Regardless of what false beliefs you have about yourself or your relationships, in whatever fears or pain you're clinging to, seek the truth. Stop taking the bait and believing the lies.

We can't keep believing in our negative beliefs and delusions. We need to accept God's truth and let it be a major part of our lives. If not, we'll fall victim to constant doubt and fear.

We need to do more than check off our daily Bible time from our to-do list, because that's just not enough.

Wake-Up Call Moments

I woke up at one point in my life and realized I had been tiptoeing for too long. I realized I wasn't doing enough to pursue God in my life. I was just going through the motions, thinking those were enough.

Are you there right now too? Many Christians I know have gone through the same yo-yo cycle I did. You aren't alone in this, but I want you to know just how important it is to solve this problem. Personally, I felt like I wasn't fully invested in my faith. I always felt like something was missing.

I was just tiptoeing. I wanted to be all in, but I just wasn't.

The problem is that when you're tiptoeing, you're not fully focused on God. You're just doing *some* of the things He expects you to do. You're following some of His convenient rules only when they work to your benefit. But you're not fully invested and engaged in who you should be and what you should be doing.

You can easily lose your faith by living like this. In truth, a genuine relationship with God is rocky. A feeling of emptiness is actually your call to God if you take the time to listen.

When it comes to the pursuit of God and your sense of identity and purpose, the list of possibilities is endless. Many red flags will show up in your life, telling you that tiptoeing with faith doesn't work. But the resolution is as simple as saying yes. With humility simply say yes to Him and all He has planned for you, everything He will give you access to.

We have been given this relationship, but it is a two-way street. We have to respond. We have to give back. We need to engage and contribute. We have to pursue Him with a childlike curiosity and vigor ... just as He pursues us. We have to be all in; we have to jump, take the step forward, take the leap of faith, and surrender, whatever the outcome is.

He is right there, waiting for us. We have to engage and take the risk, dip our toes in the water. We need to dive in and submerge ourselves.

Answer these questions to start discovering how you can transform your faith. Reflect on these questions and write down your answers if you like. Try to be descriptive.

Have you ever felt like a yo-yo Christian? How so?

Reveal the areas in your life that you are tiptoeing. Where are you holding back? What is holding you back? Why?

What are you afraid of? What doubts do you have?

List some of the steps you might take to resolve these fears and doubts.

Do you ever feel like your faith is on shaky ground? What can you do to firm up the foundation of your faith?

What will happen if you continue to tiptoe?

Are you currently tiptoeing in your faith? If so, let's talk about how you can make a difference in your life. The fact that you've recognized this is an issue in your life is a significant and powerful first step toward solving your life's problems.

Now that you've come to this realization, you need to determine how to move forward and improve your faith. I want you to choose just *one* way to spend more time with God this week. It doesn't need to be anything complicated. But I do want you to be more intentional about reading the Bible, praying, worshipping, and spending time with the one who created you.

As you focus on scripture or follow God in another way, reflect on this verse: "Your word is a lamp for my feet, a light on my path" (Psalm 119:105 NIV).

CHAPTER 4
JUST BREATHE

Come to me, all you who are weary and burdened, and I will give
you rest. Take my yoke upon you and learn from me, for I am
gentle and humble in heart, and you will find rest for your souls.

—Matthew 11:28–29 (NIV)

My day started at four o'clock in the morning when my alarm clock
went off like a blaring horn on a train barreling down the tracks. It
was a spring morning in May, and my typical busy day began. I had
a fitness class at five o'clock, and then my clients started rolling in. I
packed lunches, got the kids off to school, and kicked off my day as
usual. Finally, I headed on into the greenhouse. This was my typical
day. My husband, Rob, and I have a greenhouse and nursery. May is
the busy season. We often work sixty to eighty hours a week during
spring. After twenty years, we got used to this pace.

We simply loved working in the greenhouse. It worked for us. It took
a lot of time and energy, but we were committed to it at that point in
our lives. It didn't seem like we had any other options at that busy time
of year. There were days when I felt so exhausted that I didn't think I
could function. I felt like I was constantly running from one place to
the next. How was I supposed to keep up?

After working in the greenhouse all day, three thirty rolled around, which meant I had to pick up the kids from school. I was late picking them up as usual, always running a few minutes behind.

Nonetheless, I picked the kids up, and everything was fine. Life was crazy at that point. Anyone with young kids can relate. It was hard to keep up, but I loved my kids, and I wanted to do my best for them as any parent would.

My hectic life went on for a few years, and there are a few specific days or moments that really stand out to me amid the chaos of my everyday routine. Those included important baseball tournaments, academic milestones, and much more.

I remember this moment like it was yesterday. It stands out among all the other moments in my life while raising our kids. The kids chatted, telling me all about their school day. They smiled and giggled, full of pure joy. It was just a normal conversation during a normal car ride home from school. Well, at least for the kids, it was. I nodded and smiled with my hands at ten and two on the steering wheel.

But my mind raced. All I could think about was how I was going to get across town for baseball, get to the track meet, cook dinner with an empty fridge, grab a white T-shirt for a tie-dye day project at school, and help the kids finish their homework. I knew my husband and I wouldn't get home until nine o'clock at night.

I think I lost it after that realization. I felt overwhelmed and exhausted. From that point on, I didn't hear one word my kids said. It all went in one ear and out the other. I thought about the long list of to-dos, knowing I had to just get through that day so I could hit the repeat button again at four o'clock in the morning the next day.

I kept thinking about how being constantly busy was controlling my life. I felt like I had no control over my daily life and that I just had to roll with it.

While I loved raising my kids when they were little, I also loved working in the greenhouse, running a coaching business, and helping women.

I was doing good things in my life, but altogether it was just too much. And all those smaller, behind-the-scenes things were making my life only more stressful.

"The River" was playing on a local Christian radio station. We listen to "The River" and other Christian music, since there is no possible way to yell at our kids when listening to worship music. I always say we need to hear what we need to hear when we need to hear it. Next, the song "Breathe" by Johnny Diaz began playing. Tears started rolling down my face, and dry heaves soon followed. I listened to the lyrics and really felt them. "Just breathe."

The kids had no clue what was going on or what was wrong. "What's wrong, Mom?" they asked.

I had no response but the fake "I'm all good." At that moment, I knew I couldn't keep up living like I was, going through the motions, burning the candle at both ends, and feeling like I was spiraling out of control. I was out of control—no doubt about it.

So I took a deep breath and decided to make some changes. It was a pivotal moment. I knew I couldn't keep going on with my life the way it was, but that's all I knew. I didn't know what I was going to do or how I was going to get there.

But I knew I wasn't the only woman who felt that way.

I eventually realized I was just living in survival mode. I wanted to know how long I had been in that place and how I could make it stop. It was pure chaos, and I just wasn't happy. I knew there was something more out there for me, something bigger, happier, and less stressful. I thought, *Who can keep living like this?*

So when I got home that night, I stayed up late, trying to figure out what I could do to change my life. It wasn't an overnight fix, but I was committed to making a change in my life. I just didn't know exactly where to begin.

I chatted with my husband and my best friends to try to get some kind of clarity. I needed some type of direction, because honestly I didn't know where my life was going. I felt lost, overwhelmed, and confused. It was just too much for me to handle.

Don't forget. I was so busy that I didn't really have a lot of time to spend on getting my life back together. But I tried; little by little, I tried to juggle everything in my life. I couldn't put my kids' baseball practices, school events, and homework on hold.

After a while, it hit me. I rushed around, trying to do it all. I realized that no matter how much I got done in a day, it wouldn't bring me comfort or peace, because it just felt like an endless cycle. I worked sixty hours a week, overwhelming myself with my to-do list, and I still felt unfulfilled. I was just going through the motions, trying to push through the day, losing sleep, rushing around, and trying to keep up with it all. I thought I had no other options as a working mom. How was I supposed to completely transform my life when it revolved around my kids?

After doing some reflecting, I knew it was definitely time for a change. I mean, I had known it before, but now I really focused on it. It motivated me to dig even deeper and figure out what I was supposed to do. I wanted to know why my life wasn't fulfilling and why I felt out of control. And it was a pivotal moment. I knew something had to change because I felt stretched so thin in my body, mind, and soul.

So what was missing?

I finally discovered that the life I was living couldn't give me the peace and contentment I was yearning for. It was pretty much out of my control. So where did I find real peace?

God.

I've always been a believer, but I wasn't all in like I should've been. For much of my life, I was a yo-yo Christian, going up and down. Sometimes I felt committed, and at other times I failed. While that's fairly normal, this gray area of faith didn't feel right to me. It led to a lot of different issues in my life.

Over time, I learned I was still missing true peace and contentment, no matter how I lived my life. I thought working those long hours and making plenty of money were enough to bring me peace. After all, they meant I didn't have to worry about much financially. I thought that running my kids to all their activities would give me peace and make me feel like a good mother.

Not only was my busy lifestyle affecting my faith and my connection to God, but it was also preventing me from being present. Looking back, I know I missed out on so many important moments in my life and my kids' lives too. I wasn't able to be fully present because of all the stress and anxiety I carried. I was constantly on the go and never had a break. So I was always stressed out.

Once I started focusing on God, I began to feel more peace, contentment, and fulfillment. I discovered that God gives the ultimate peace, which has held true no matter what my life looked like. If I was busy all the time, I felt overwhelmed. If I was slowing down, I felt like I wasn't doing enough or wasn't fulfilling my purpose.

By realizing how much peace God provides, I focused on that instead of attaching my sense of self-worth to how much I was working. I felt encouraged to pour more time into God so I could really feel peace. After that, I was able to experience an overall shift in my life. I felt less stressed. I felt less overwhelmed. I was still living out my purpose by raising my family and helping women. But life felt much different than it had before. Something had shifted in me.

Wake-Up Call Moments

I reached a moment in my life that led me to follow God more deeply, more authentically. It hit me. I needed to focus on God and the peace He provided. But I couldn't feel that peace because I always let my busy lifestyle and constant stress get in the way.

You can probably think of times in your life that lacked peace. You might not feel like your life is very peaceful right now. Maybe your schedule is jam-packed, and you can barely eat three meals a day. How are you supposed to fit God into that kind of schedule? I get it.

You aren't going to find peace in your life by making six figures a year, getting that promotion, or doing anything else. Real peace comes with faith in God and a relationship with Jesus. Do you agree?

All the things we experience in life can take that peace and joy away. So we need to keep coming back to God to preserve our sense of peace.

I want you to think this over for a moment. If you're currently lacking peace in your life and feel like you can't take the time to breathe, it's time to change that problem. Start by answering these questions and reflect on your answers. Think about how you might respond to these questions a few years from now.

What really brings you peace?

What emotions do you experience when you feel like peace is missing from your life?

Think back to a time in your life when you felt peace while focusing on God. Did God bring you peace? In what ways?

What are you willing to sacrifice to find everlasting peace? Is it judgement from others? Friends? Pray about it and answer here.

I know it's hard to feel peace in such a busy world. We all feel that way at some point in our lives. But I've found that the time we do make for Him frees up more time, more space; and it helps us approach the time we do have in a completely different light.

You still need to pay the bills and provide for your family, of course. But you can experience true peace. You can slow down.

I thought I was the busiest person on the planet with five kids while working and juggling all that life threw at me. You probably have your own busy lifestyle, which makes the idea of finding peace impossible. Maybe you've just come to that realization.

No matter what, it's time to start experiencing true peace. I want you to commit to coming back to God when you need peace in your life. When you feel overwhelmed, busy, and out of control, spend some time with God and find your peace.

We're all different and feel peace in unique ways. For you, it might come from spending time alone with the Lord, prayer and meditation. Others like to read the Bible or listen to a Christian podcast. Find what brings you peace and pursue it.

As you go about your day, think of this verse: "May the God of hope fill you with all joy and peace as you trust in Him, so that you may overflow with hope by the power of the Holy Spirit" (Romans 15:13 NIV).

CHAPTER 5
SURRENDERING AND RELEASING

Therefore do not worry about tomorrow, for tomorrow will
worry about itself. Each day has enough trouble of its own.

—Matthew 6:34 (NIV)

Most of us know we can control only two things in life: our attitude
and our effort. But that dynamic between feeling in control or losing
control often controls our lives. Our ability to control our lives plays
a huge role in how things pan out. Just thinking about that makes me
feel anxious. I know that no matter how hard I try, there will always
be things I can't control. It's definitely not easy for me to fully accept
that fact.

Call me a recovering "obsessor" of details. And when I say "recovering,"
I mean it is still a process I haven't yet mastered fully. It requires
daily, intentional effort. I lived my life on my pride, self-confidence,
self-perception, and ego. And to be truthful, my sense of value had
everything to do with what I could do independently.

From my point of view, strength meant I didn't need any help. I told
myself, "I've got this. I can do it all." I was obsessed with feeling in
control, which isn't something I like to shout from the rooftops, but it
needs to be shared. I'm all about being honest here. I want to share the
real me, whether it's good or bad. Odds are, though, you can relate. I
wanted to fix things, solve challenges, and have everything organized,

neat, and clean (even my closet was color coded). I wanted to create perfect schedules, and I needed every day to go smoothly, like this perfectly wrapped "life in a box" I had created.

And when things didn't go as planned and became chaotic (which is naturally a part of life), I didn't know how to handle it. I felt out of control, simply because I couldn't control certain things in life. So while I felt "out of control," things weren't as bad as I had made them out to be. If a client quit coaching services, there was a technical breakdown with work, or a dirty glass lingered in the sink, I'd roll my eyes, take deep breaths, and begin my mental tirade of snide remarks. You know exactly what I am talking about ... stomping through the house, letting everyone know I was annoyed.

Many emotions coursed through my body—the worry, the fear, the frustration, and frankly, a little bit of crazy. But the root of it all stemmed from needing to feel in control all the time. I was really good at hiding this drive for the most part. Still, you can imagine what my heart felt like with this constant burden of anxiety I inflicted on myself whenever I felt like I was losing control.

It didn't matter what the situation was, no matter how trivial or serious it was objectively. I needed to be in control. I felt that if I wasn't in control, everything would go terribly wrong. I felt like I needed to call the shots, or my whole life would fall apart. I had always been in control, and I never knew anything different, and I felt like this method was the only way my life could work.

Now, what about the control we want over our kids? I could go on forever about controlling their daily lives, their behavior—goodness, it could even be the subject of my next book. Naturally, we tend to do that as mamas. I know that sounds so harsh, but it is easier to see more clearly in hindsight than when you are in the thick of it all.

I know deep down that I should let go and let my children make their own decisions. I know they are unique individuals and that I don't have control over their lives. But as I said, I've always been obsessed with details. And as a person who feels the most comfortable when in control, I thought I had to be in charge of every aspect of my life and theirs, because they were constantly in my orbit and responsibility.

Someone once asked me, "Would you rather be in the toddler phase or the teenage years?"

Without hesitation, I said, "The toddler phase all the way!" With teenagers, we are ultimately unable to control their choices as they gain independence and learn to become young adults. Are they texting and driving? Drinking? Vaping? Doing drugs? Whom are they hanging out with? Is there a girlfriend or boyfriend in the picture? Did they finish their homework? Are they coming home by curfew?

The list goes on and on and on … everything I had little to no control over. This letting go was hard on me. I couldn't control everything in their lives if I wanted them to become mature adults and feel safe and loved unconditionally.

I didn't literally announce to everyone that I was in control or that I was the boss; to be honest, looking back, I'm not even sure I could admit to myself that my problems stemmed from needing to be in control. I just chalked them up to having high expectations and determination, which felt like a good thing. I felt like I was just someone who liked to crush goals and have a role to live up to. I thought it was part of being a wife, a mom of five, and a highly driven woman. I like organization and structure, and there is nothing wrong with that. Don't get me wrong. These are all good things to have in the right measure … until they rob your peace and chip away at your sanity and joy until they become compulsive.

I hung onto everything I thought I could, trying to control the outcomes and results of pretty much everything. I can tell you straight up from experience that we can't have total control over our paths in life. It doesn't fit in a perfectly wrapped gift box with a pretty big bow on it. Life can change in an instant, yet I was doing everything in my power to defy the odds to create and control a perfect life. The control showed up as perfectionism. After thirty-plus years of perfecting perfectionism, I finally learned to let go of controlling every single detail of my life; and let me tell you, it's still a challenge. Learning to let go takes work.

But I had to learn to let go and ask for help. Needing to feel in control was itself controlling my life. But for a long time, learning to ask for help sounded weak to me. Yet I had to be okay with that and allow my heart to open up to the possibility that I wasn't meant to carry all this weight on my shoulders, that asking for help from Him was actually a sign of inner strength. I was carrying a load that wasn't my burden to carry. I had to shift the focus from me to Him. I began seeking Him and all this inexplicable peace others were talking about and living their lives with. I desperately wanted to feel that, to join in on the secret to living they all shared.

I didn't want to feel weighed down anymore, but that would require me to let go and surrender everything to Him, a source I couldn't see … to a God I believed was real. But that belief required that I walk with obedience in faith. I had to not only hear Him but also listen to His word and how it spoke through my entire life. I had to listen with the trust that He would take care of me and my life.

Coming to that realization was difficult. But once I gave my life over to God and let Him take full control of my life, I realized just how silly it had been for me to feel this need to be in control for so long. I had to let go of a life I was trying to create, force, and fit into this ideal picture, which revolved around my unrealistic time frame and how I wanted things done. I had to step back from my expectations of myself and let God take over with His plan for me. I had to go with His flow.

I'm laughing as I write this. Me? Going with the flow? Me? Handing everything over to God? Surrendering? Talk about a wake-up call from the carefully crafted identity I had spent so many years building. I wasn't being honest with myself, but that doesn't mean I had given up on my goals or dreams by going with the flow and God's path for me. I'm just simply putting my trust and faith in the bigger and better plan God has for me.

So I encourage you to relax and surrender rather than to resist and question the life that was meant for you. So do you want more from your life? Do you want to get everything you truly want in life?

Things We Can Let Go Of

I've learned to stop obsessing over the details and micromanaging every aspect of my life. I've accepted that there are things I can let go of. It hasn't been easy to (1) admit that I need to let go of anything and to (2) find things to let go of.

Instead of taking on the overwhelming thought of giving all my control over to God, I try to focus on the smaller things I need to let go of daily, one at a time. Small tasks have become more manageable because I don't let go of everything all at once. Learning to let go has become a process, not something to tackle all at once.

As I've been working on losing control in my life—in a good way—I've focused on the following areas of my life. These are all things I've either let go of or am working on letting go of. And they are all things you can let go of too.

Guilt

There are plenty of moments in our lives that make us feel guilty. When we hold onto that guilt and don't release it, it controls our lives. We may feel guilty for missing an event at work, and we worry about what everyone else thinks of us for skipping it. So guilt tends to control our actions. In a constant catch-up game, we might strive to prove ourselves to others to manage that guilt.

Shame

We've all made choices we're ashamed about. If we don't let go of the shame, then we continue to let it guide our future choices. To avoid future shame, we keep things private or don't make the choices we actually want to make. We might feel embarrassed, and we don't want to let people down.

Perfection

I've battled with perfection myself. I would consider myself a perfectionist. The problem with perfectionism is that it sneaks its way into everything I do and takes control of every aspect of my life. I feel like I can't make my own decisions or do things differently because everything needs to be perfect.

I was obsessed with keeping in order. I couldn't handle a dirty dish in the sink. And my pillows on the couch and the bed were always tidy and straight. You're probably thinking I'm crazy, but keeping things orderly was my morning routine to get ready for my day. I work from home, so a perfect environment was essential to me. My husband, Rob, will intentionally leave crumbs on the counter or walk by the bed and dishevel the pillows just to see if I move them back. That went on for years before I realized it was him messing with me and not an oversight on my part. I realized he was playing a joke on me. But one day, I left the pillows crooked on purpose because I was becoming self-aware of the controlling perfectionist I was trying to be.

Negativity

Negative thoughts can easily take over our lives. When we constantly tell ourselves we aren't good enough, that becomes our truth, and it's hard to break free from it. When I focus on the things I think I'm not good at or the things I'm doing wrong in my life, I create a vicious cycle that's hard to escape.

People Who Tear Us Down

There are always going to be people in our lives who try to tear us down. Whether it's behind a computer screen or in person, these actions hurt. And those words or actions can start to creep in and influence the decisions we make every day. They can control how we live our lives. We start to believe they're true, even when they absolutely are not.

Worry and Anxiety

It's normal to feel anxious or worry from time to time. The problem is when this feeling begins to take control of our lives. At some point, we start making decisions out of fear instead of logic. We start to believe our fears are justified and based on truth. As a mom, there's a long list of things I could be worried about. But by surrendering it all to God, I have been able to let God control my worries instead of letting my worries control me.

What Others Think

I used to think about what others thought of me. I used to worry about being good enough in their eyes. As you can probably imagine, this anxiety began to play a role in my life. I made too many decisions based on what others might think of me. I missed out on opportunities because I was afraid someone would think I was weird, crazy, or stupid. Now my only focus is on how I look in God's eyes.

Overwhelm

It's easy to feel overwhelmed in our lives. As a mom, I know how busy my life can be. I run from one thing to the next while still trying to take care of myself and my home, business, marriage, and so much more. For a while, I lived in a constant state of being overwhelmed, and trust me, that's no way to live. How could I go on like that?

Wake-Up Call Moments

How do you feel about your need to control right now? Do you feel like you need to be in control, or do you let God control your life? Be honest with yourself.

I know it was really hard for me to surrender that control. If you're anything like me, it probably won't be easy for you either, but it's so worth it.

Maybe you can think of a specific time in your life when things felt out of your control. When I think about those moments, I feel uncomfortable. I know God had control of my life, but I didn't know that back then.

If you want to experience peace in your life, you have to let go of the need to control your life. You need to move past the unrealistic expectation that everything is in your hands—because it's not. It's in God's hands.

If you're currently trying to surrender control, you need to really dig deep and let go. You need to accept the idea of surrender—not just as a concept but as something that takes faith, willpower, work, and intent. You need to look at your heart and at what God wants for your life.

Take a moment and reflect on these questions. Jot down your answers, pray about them, or talk through them with a friend or your spouse. Hopefully, this exercise will give you some clarity.

What in your life have you not fully handed over to God to take control of?

How do you feel about the idea of God being in control of your life? Why do you feel this way?

What are you willing to hand over to God right now?

How do you feel about the idea of God being in control of your life? Why do you feel this way?

How do you think surrendering control would benefit your life?

What are three reasons you're hesitant to surrender control?

I know firsthand that letting go is hard. I know that it feels natural and easier to be in control. You feel safe when you're in control. But the truth is, we're safer when God's in control.

To help you loosen the reins, try to focus on one area of your life at a time. You might feel overwhelmed by trying to fully surrender your life to God all at once. God doesn't ask you to go all in all at once but to take the first step. It's okay to make mistakes as long as you get back up and try again. God doesn't ask that you be perfect; He asks that you be present and do the work to change your life. In little moments of your life where you're trying to take control, step back and pray to God. Ask Him to take control instead.

If you trust in God, you can trust Him to take control of your life and take care of you and your family.

Throughout the day, reflect on this verse: "Have I not commanded you? Be strong and courageous. Do not be afraid; do not be discouraged, for the LORD your God will be with you wherever you go" (Joshua 1:9 NIV).

CHAPTER 6
OVERCOMING

I have told you these things, so that in me you may
have peace. In this world you will have trouble.
But take heart! I have overcome the world.

—John 16:33 (NIV)

I love to run. I love to push my body and compete with myself. It feels so good to accomplish my goals and know I've overcome all my fears and doubts to get there. To this day, I compete with myself whenever I can. I try to find ways to push myself and to overcome anything that comes my way.

I love to challenge myself to beat my personal best time or to go just one extra mile. I love to see what I can do with my body and how I can push myself mentally. Doing this has only encouraged me to keep pushing myself. It's made me faster and stronger.

Listen up, though. I haven't always been like this. I didn't always love running long distances or trying to beat my record. My records embarrassed me compared to everyone else's. I didn't think I was good enough. And I thought it would be too much work to get to where I wanted to be. What a change compared to where I am today. It's like night and day.

I remember wanting to run on my terms, and when the distance became too long or too hard, I began to struggle. I just quit. I went out for the high school cross-country team all four years, and guess what? I quit all four times. I was a coach's favorite. It's hard for me to figure out that I became a collegiate runner and ran marathons and ultras. I became an Ironwoman, and I've logged thousands of miles since then. I still train for events today. Running is truly a part of who I am. What goes through your mind when someone quits cross-country but loves to train, compete, and race? The point is to overcome self-doubt and to reach a place of genuine self-confidence and personal growth.

I think back to one race in particular. It was the Ironman in Hawaii, my first attempt at conquering 140.6 miles. I recall the excitement of treading water in the crystal-clear blue water on the coast of Kona, Hawaii. Swimming straight out 1.2 miles into the ocean, where the fear of sharks, faster competitors swimming past you, and getting kicked in the face (or you kicking others) was all just part of the excitement of the competition. I know, it sounds scary. But I was amped up. This was the moment for which I'd been planning for what felt like forever. When the chaos and the nerves from the cannon fire subsided, everything went quiet. All I heard was the sound of my breath and my racing thoughts. And the silence beneath the water. I just kept swimming. I soaked it all in, knowing I was creating a memory that would always stay with me.

This was something you don't do every day. I felt a flood of emotions. I felt confident that I could do this. After all, I had been training for this moment. I was just getting started, but I was excited. I thought I had the mental and physical strength to complete the whole Ironman. We hit the navy ship turnaround point and started to swim back toward the beach for another 1.2 miles. I made it. That first part of the race gave me a good boost of confidence to keep going. But I knew in my mind it was only the beginning.

Soaking wet and climbing off the beach, I started to run toward the bike transition. Smiling all the way, waving to all the spectators, and stripping the wetsuit off as I jogged in to find my bike among thousands, I was ready to take on the 112-mile bike course. I had spent months training for this race. Years, really. Being disciplined and showing up every day no matter what had prepared me for this day. I hopped on the bike, clipped my shoes in, refueled, and took off.

The first fifty-six miles were surreal and fast. My quads pounded it out, and the sun got hotter as the hours passed by. After five hours on the bike, my body started to feel the heat. The 110-degree, black lava pavement raced past me. Add in the fifty-mile-per-hour crosswind, and my mind started to go haywire. I was literally in the fire.

The enemy and negative thoughts crept in. *You are not going to make it. You look tired. Are you sure this is worth the pain?* Every negative thought played on repeat in my head, playing games with me, taunting me. Throwing in the towel seemed easier. I started questioning whether I had it in me. I thought I was crazy for signing up for this insane competition in the first place, convinced I would never make it.

But in that moment of heavy breathing and sweat and pain, there was no way I was going to quit. That day, I would be an Ironman. I remember seeing my three-year-old son, Hayden, and my husband on that corner at mile 112, and my heart felt uplifted. Hayden's "Go Mommy" sign was just what I needed at that exact moment. That jolt of love and support put the wind back in my sails—perfect timing at the end of the bike race and my charge into the 26.2-mile run.

Yep, there was a full marathon to finish the race. "This is it," I told myself. "I've got this." I love running. This was my strongest leg of the race. I have done tons of marathons. No problem. Homestretch. Every step of that 26.2 miles took every ounce of energy I had left. One moment I felt great, all in stride and clipping off the miles. The next minute, I wanted to cry from the pain, exhaustion, and hunger.

The impossible odds of me finishing this race started to gnaw at me. I knew I wasn't the only competitor out there feeling the pressure. This was a hard race, no matter how much time we had put into training. I'm sure everyone in the race had some doubts and moments of weakness. Who wouldn't? It wasn't meant to be easy.

I knew I needed to shift my focus. The pity party just wasn't working. I started to shift the focus off myself and onto others. My coaching instinct started to kick in. This is what I do for a living, so I have tons of experience helping people through challenges. Until this moment, I didn't know just how important it was for me to cheer others on, not just myself. I focused on them and boosted them up as we were all in this together. We were not alone. We were all out there to test our physical limits, to test our mental and emotional limits, and ultimately to test our faith, to run this race to the best of our abilities.

Twilight came, and by the eleventh hour, it was dark. The elite athletes had long since finished. There were just the ordinary, average competitors still on the course, taking one step in front of the other. Even if I was just an ordinary, average competitor, I knew I could push through and do this. I didn't care what place I came in or how quickly I finished. I set my mind on being the cheerleader and finishing the Ironman.

I remember the moment I shifted my mindset. It was amazing when I started to shift my focus on others and notice what I was telling myself at that moment. My pace started to pick up. I felt a boost in my energy. My outlook brightened. Giving up wasn't an option. I overcame all the pain and discomfort simply with a mental shift. I knew I would finish, no matter what. I would reach a personal victory. I had missed the importance of this mentality for so much of the race in energy and stamina. But it hit me at just the right time. If it hadn't, I don't know how I would have hit the finish line. I might not have finished the race if my mindset hadn't shifted at just the right time.

Twelve hours and seventeen minutes later, I entered the final straightaway. My son had fallen asleep on the curb, using the "Go, Mommy" sign as a mat, and my husband still cheered me on as loudly as he could. Tears fell down my face as I sprinted in as fast as I could through a tunnel of screaming fans. I crossed that line, and the announcer said, "Congratulations, Jill … You are an Ironman."

I was so proud of myself. I had done it. This was the moment I had been waiting for.

I didn't realize just how meaningful it would be to hear my name announced on a loudspeaker. It made my achievement concrete in real time. I mean, I had known it would be special. I had worked hard and had something to show for it. I had overcome the odds. I had ignored the negative self-doubt constantly chattering in my head.

When I heard my name announced, when I heard that I was finally an Ironman, I thought about God speaking those words to me. I thought about God telling me I was a "chosen one." I thought about how much I meant to God and that He had been able to help me overcome one of the greatest challenges in my life.

That message translates to other parts of my life too. Accomplishing the Ironman was a personal and spiritual fight. I worked my butt off while training for the race, putting in endless hours each week. Then, when it was my time to shine, I put in the effort and put myself to the test—both mentally and physically.

Now I have to fight the good fight for God, the ultimate test. I have to stand firm in my faith, no matter what happens in life. I can overcome whatever might come my way by the grace of God.

All my pain, self-doubt, and exhaustion diminished once I finished that race. And all I could do was smile and reflect on such a special day—a race I will always remember. The long days of training. Months of discipline. The ups and downs and commitment one takes to run the race.

This connects to our spiritual lives too. There are going to be ups and downs in our faith. There are going to be times when we need God to help us overcome the challenges we face. Of course, I know I need God all the time. I can't live life without Him. I can't pick and choose when I need Him, but I especially need Him in those dark and challenging times.

I went through a lot during training. I can't even count the number of hours I put in. It was a huge commitment to train for something as important as Ironman. But everything I had done finally paid off.

Of all the races I have run with an eye toward the finish line, I cannot help but think it all pales in comparison to the "journey of life" Jesus has set before us. It is a journey intended to strengthen our spiritual faith. God has called on us to take part in that journey at our own pace, at our own time and will, in every moment. Do we realize it's a path of ups and downs, of personal training, not the "finish line," that defines who we are? Are we training for our God-given goals and purpose? How long does it take until we reach that breakthrough? Do we quit when it gets hard?

We can't know when a blow will hit our family, when a rocky spot will hit our marriage, or when our kids will push back and challenge us. We can't anticipate when a friend will betray us or abandon us, when our career will hit a slump, or when the illness or sudden death of a loved one will strike out of the blue. God cannot guarantee calm waters at every moment, but He *can* give us the strength and faith to overcome them. Life isn't about perfection and control but about overcoming adversity and discovering our personal strength.

That journey of life is the most important task God will ever ask you to undertake. It can feel like a race, a paddle, a yawn, or a stagnant activity, but it's always a *journey*, and it's always at a pace meant for you. God will never give you more than you can handle. We will always face challenges in life, and we need to overcome them. We can't give up when things get hard or when we deny the voice of God whispering in our ear.

What's "hard" for you? What "fire" are you walking through? What are you supposed to do? Do you lose faith or give up on your calling?

Do you face that mountain and turn back? Or do you keep going and tackle every challenge put in front of you? Do you overcome it? Do you refuse to give up?

I totally get it. Going full throttle and listening to God's will for you can be confusing and exhausting. Maybe you haven't discovered that call yet, but you need to hold on, refuse to give up, and believe that faith has the power to overcome every obstacle the devil tries to throw your way. And believe me, he likes to throw obstacles in your way and dish out lies, which seem like your own thoughts, to keep you down. But we need to pick ourselves up from those lows when life gets tough. We aren't meant to stay in a place of stagnation and self-doubt.

We are called to rise up like mighty warriors. We aren't just being called; we are given strength through Him. I had to train for the Ironman on my own. I had to put in the hours, miles, sweat, and tears. When it comes to reaching victory in Jesus, we don't need to gain that strength. God gives it to us. God helps us to trust in Him to help us achieve our personal victories.

Jesus has always called us to strive beyond all odds and overcome adversity. We must stay steady in the race of life, which is ultimately a race against our own self-imposed limitations. We will inevitably face hurt, pain, rejection, ridicule, and struggle in life. Sometimes we feel like we have nothing left to give. It is in those moments when we must turn to the Lord. He will empower us to stand strong, to keep going. In those moments, we should harness the power of God and our faith in Him to stay the course.

I have thrown in the towel and quit at times, but God has promised us that we shall reap the rewards according to His divine timing and through our own free will and intention. He urges us to overcome at every moment of our lives. He urges us to keep going to win the race He has challenged us to win.

No matter what comes our way, God is on our side. He's there to help us overcome the ups and downs of life—and everything in between.

He will give us the strength we need to stay steadfast with full faith in Him. Nothing can separate us from God. Our strength comes from Him, no matter how we struggle. The race can bring illness, death, a job loss, or any other tragedy. But true strength lies in our faith that God will carry us through these adversities.

We know God is good. We know He has the power to give us life. We know He is with us. We know we will never need to overcome anything on our own.

Think about the areas of your life where you struggle to reach the finish line. It is through your faith and belief that you will thrive on your journey.

Wake-Up Call Moments

Are you currently struggling to overcome something? Do you feel like you're fighting this battle alone?

It's easy to feel alone in life. It's easy to feel like you're trying to figure everything out for yourself with no help from anyone else. When it comes to overcoming those challenges in your life, there's only one way to do it that actually works.

When I was running the Ironman, I had my doubts. I wondered whether I could truly finish the race. I wondered whether I could overcome all the fears and doubts that flooded my mind. Of course, deep down I knew I had put in serious training to prepare for these twelve hours of my life. But when the time came, doubt set in.

We struggle with so many things in our lives. I'm the first to admit quitting is the easy way out.

But when we overcome these things through Christ, our trust in Him is strengthened. We know we can call on Him to deliver us from anything that comes our way.

I want you to reflect for a moment on the following questions. But it's important to be actively present as you ponder over them. Don't just work through them to get them done like they are homework. Dig a little deeper and look into your heart.

What is a situation God has helped you to overcome? Think back to a specific time and how God stood by you.

```


```

What is something you gave up on instead of trusting God to help you overcome the challenge? How would your life be different if you conquered that challenge with God's help?

```


```

List three things you wish to overcome in your life right now. These can be big or small problems.

```


```

What are some of the things you tell yourself when you're considering giving up? How do you think God would respond to your doubt? What would He say?

What do you hope to gain by overcoming these challenges with God on your side?

There's no guarantee that our lives are going to be easy. We face so many challenges in our lives. Life isn't meant to be easy. But that isn't the point. Challenges will come, whether you like them or not. You can't prevent bad things from happening. But you *can* change your attitude and your belief to ease your transition through them.

You can count on God to help you through anything that might happen in your life. You don't have to do this alone. You don't need to give up when life gets hard.

God is on your side and will walk you through the battles so you can be victorious through Christ.

I want you to walk away with an important verse. This verse reminds me that God can help us overcome anything to gain that victory: "Not that I have already obtained all this, or have already arrived at my goal, but I press on to take hold of that for which Christ Jesus took hold of me. Brothers and sisters, I do not consider myself yet to have taken hold of it. But one thing I do: Forgetting what is behind and straining toward what is ahead, I press on toward the goal to win the prize for which God has called me heavenward in Christ Jesus" (Philippians 3:12–14 NIV).

CHAPTER 7
QUIT GETTING OFFENDED

A person's wisdom yields patience; it is to
one's glory to overlook an offense.

—Proverbs 19:11 (NIV)

You know when you're on the airplane, and people start plowing their way up to the front? The coach ditchers? You know who I'm talking about. You wonder, *Where do they think they're going?* Let me tell you, I used to be a "ditcher," and I can't judge. A storm delayed my flight to Chicago, and my connecting flight cut it really close. But I had to make that flight heading to Dublin, Ireland. There was no way I could miss it. I was no joke in the plane's last corner seat since I always fly the cheapest seat available.

You know how Chicago is; it takes you an hour just to get to another terminal. Well, here I was on repeat. "Excuse me, so sorry. I have a flight to catch." Oh, you should have seen the glaring, judgmental stares I got. They didn't care about my dilemma.

One woman stood her ground and wouldn't let me through. I was stuck. She told me I had to wait my turn. I felt offended. There could have been a scene if I had lost my temper. I missed my flight to Ireland.

Have you ever taken offense from the actions or words of others? Yeah, I haven't either. Just kidding! Of course, we all have. Guilty, right here.

I'll bet you are holding on to something right now, and you may not even realize it. You may be holding onto that offense, and you may have to dig deep to find it. We may need to face some things and let go of our pride to deal with the truth. We may be in a trap and held a prisoner, not truly understanding we can ultimately escape from it and be free.

Sometimes we don't realize we can live our lives differently. We don't always realize there's another way to react or treat people or let go of old grievances. Sometimes we get stuck in old patterns because of how we were raised or how we see others behaving as we grow up. We come to assume we don't need to change our perspective.

But it's so important to change our perspective over time, to do things differently, to challenge our perceptions and how we react, and not to take offense but to just notice. It's important to realize we can do things differently. We don't always need to react the same way like we're on autopilot.

What I've learned over the years is that there's always a reason we take offense. There are underlying reasons that make us feel this way, mainly through our childhood and ingrained beliefs. This is totally normal, but it shouldn't be. Does God want us to take offense?

Let's take a more in-depth look into our hearts. We'll undoubtedly find bitterness, resentment, and anger still lingering. If we look even deeper, we might find envy, hurt, and strife going on, any of which can turn a heart that was once filled with love and joy into stone. You may even feel it hardening each day that you cling to past hurts, pain, and offenses. You can probably think of specific situations that contribute to those feelings.

I'm guessing you don't want to take an in-depth look. You probably felt betrayed, wronged, or mistreated. A friend turned his or her back. A marriage failed. A relationship disintegrated. Someone you cared for deeply offended or hurt you. Someone gossiped about you or criticized you. How dare he or she say that to you? How could he or she do that? You are so innocent in the face of his or her betrayal. Is that what you want to hear? Does it make you feel better? Does your conviction that you are the victim justify your attitude and behavior?

I'm betting it doesn't. Let me speak from experience. Playing the victim and holding onto any offense won't make you feel any better. You will still feel trapped, hurt, and pinned down by the enemy while wallowing in self-pity. You'll only be held back from all God has planned for you.

When you think about all the things that have influenced how you respond to other people's words and actions, I'm sure you feel like you can justify your offense. But you are more likely focusing on how negative it all makes you feel toward a sense of self-serving vindication. Even if you don't think about what makes you feel offended, it can linger and hit you later. That's the danger of feeling offense, and it has no place when it comes to our faith in God and letting go.

You might wonder why someone did or said something offensive. You might wonder how he or she was capable of something so needless, senseless, or just plain cruel.

I totally get it. When we have expectations of how others should behave and that doesn't happen, taking offense and feeling hurt come easily. The reality is that everyone has to make his or her own decisions in life, knowing full well how decisions and choices affect others. Someone making the wrong decision can easily offend us and make us unhappy.

Life gives us plenty of opportunities to get sucked into trials and distorts our vision and hearts. Remember, the enemy is trying to take us down. God tells us about this and how we should respond. "But I say to you, love your enemies, bless those who curse you, do good to those who hate you, and pray for those who spitefully use you and persecute you" (Matthew 5:44 NIV).

That lesson doesn't seem hard in concept, but it is in practice in everyday life. It doesn't make sense. I know it didn't work for me when I was faced with a decision. The "good Jill" wanted to be kind. But the hurt and angry Jill had no interest in goodwill toward others. It is in our human nature to fight for our survival. To protect. To get revenge. To build a wall around our hearts so we don't get hurt. That is the reality for most of us, but it is a fundamentally self-centered attitude.

Getting offended is a natural by-product of being upset. But that's not what God wants. That's not how He wants us to treat others or feel about others. He doesn't want us to fall for that instant gratification of "offense" without forethought. After all, we're called, first and foremost, to treat others with kindness and compassion before any misgivings, doubt, or fear ever enters the picture.

"You have heard that it was said, 'Eye for eye and tooth for tooth.' But I tell you, do not resist an evil person. If anyone slaps you on the right cheek, turn to them the other cheek also. And if anyone wants to sue you and take your shirt, hand over your coat as well" (Matthew 5:38–40 NIV).

Before I knew my identity in Christ, surrendering and turning the other cheek felt weak. And feeling weak doesn't feel good, and it wasn't something I wanted to look like or feel since it wasn't the norm, nor encouraged or praised by our cultural standards. Do you blame me? Maybe you can relate. We have been taught to hold our own, to not be taken advantage of, to take control of our lives. We keep playing the broken record of deceit and mistreatment. We repeatedly blame ourselves for lost vindication and validation as proof that we were wronged. We empower that root of bitterness to gain a stronghold in our hearts, where love and forgiveness should live instead.

But as I said, I had this problem before I knew my identity in Christ and what I needed to truly focus on. And it certainly wasn't the rejection, negativity, or betrayal of others that led me to Christ. I am here to tell you that there's something better than fighting back and taking offense. Our faith increases in Him by turning the other cheek and blessing our enemies; our faith is increased in Him. I get it that faith doesn't feel natural or even right. It doesn't make sense most of the time. It sounds crazy. But imagine the greater good. There is something better.

71

Revenge or resentment doesn't heal the heart. Playing hardball doesn't fix the wrongs. We've all heard that two wrongs don't make a right.

While growing up, I remember the friend who was always late for practice and the last to be picked up. Her mom was never on time. She always got caught up in other things. She forgot the pickup time or something else as she was running out the door. As a kid, I thought, *Why is she always late? Why is she so irresponsible? How hard can it be?* I always felt sorry for her despite my judgment. It was so embarrassing in junior high to be the straggler, whose mom was always late to pick her up.

The vision of her mom peeling around the corner in her van, her hair pulled back in a ponytail, the door flying open, and kids jumping out and sprinting into the school still remains with me today. But now I totally get it, because I realize I am that mom!

Most Saturdays, I have to be at five different places at once. Track meets, basketball games, baseball practices, fundraisers—and I am sure there's something else I'm forgetting. I usually pull in five minutes before game time and kick the kids out of the car, tie shoelaces, pull hair into rough ponytails, and sprint to the gym—normal daily life we've gotten used to. We somehow make it all work with five kids. No judging here!

Now I totally understand where her mom was coming from. Her dropping off my teammate late as a kid now seems like no big deal; in fact, it seems trivial, and she's become my hero.

Here's the thing. We can't know what people are really going through. I've challenged myself to think about what others might be going through and why they may feel the way they do. But unless I'm standing in their shoes, I can only guess.

I want you to think about a few scenarios. Was the lady who wouldn't let me through in the airport just tired of being taken advantage of, so she held me off? Did the rude checkout lady at the grocery store have a fight with her husband right before her shift? Was the speedy driver who cut you off on the highway rushing to the hospital to say goodbye to a loved one? Was the lady who didn't say hi to you in the store barely hanging on by a thread—a busy and overwhelmed mom? Was the road-rage guy filled with bitterness, anger, and hurt? Did they cause him to go off at a minor offense?

We have no idea. Of course, we can focus on the fact that these people were rude and inconsiderate, and we can easily take offense, or we can look through a different lens. I'm sure we have all judged, taken offense, and daily had certain expectations of others. That's just part of life. But what happens when the issue hits closer to home and closer to the heart? A relationship that means the world to you gets broken and feels like the ultimate betrayal. These are the things we keep private, keep personal, and hold close to our hearts. How many of us are walking around with these burdens?

I know I have walked around with so many of these heavy feelings for years. It takes a lot of effort to release them. And I know it's hard to work through these issues sometimes. When you think about the weight you have on your shoulders, it isn't always easy to go through the process of releasing yourself of that weight.

By this time in your life, you've had at least a few things to overcome. You've had to work through so many ups and downs. You know working through them isn't simple, so it can be discouraging to think about everything else you still need to improve in your life.

The point is that this journey is totally worth it. Why? Because it's what God wants for us. He wants us to stop taking offense and to respond with love and kindness. He wants us to be gentle with ourselves.

Wake-Up Call Moments

Think about how easily you might take offense. Do you let things get to you, no matter how big or small?

I know it's not easy to stop taking offense. It's taken me a while to figure this out for myself, and I still struggle with it sometimes. What really made a difference is the mindset I have toward others.

You can probably think of several times in your life when you've let those feelings of offense get the best of you and influence your actions or reactions. We've all been there.

To help you think about when you take offense and why this happens, work through these questions. I encourage you to spend a little bit of time on these questions and not rush through them.

What hurts are you holding on to?

What triggers these hurts and the pain that comes with them?

Who needs forgiveness in your life? Is it you? Is it someone else? (Whether they deserve it or not, who needs it?)

Dig deep: What part of your heart needs healing to be set free?

Who has offended you? How have you turned the other cheek? How have you not?

What about you? How have you hurt others? Whom do you need forgiveness from? Why?

What needs to change within you?

In the Bible, God urges us to be kind and compassionate. He wants us to care about others, just like He cares about us. He wants us to forgive each other, just like He has forgiven us.

What we need to do is heal, forgive, and be obedient. We need to see people through God's eyes instead of filtering everything through past hurts, rejections, and experiences. We are not the judge, so we need to treat others with compassion and give grace.

Think back to this verse throughout the day and try to replace those feelings of offense with compassion. "Be kind and compassionate to one another, forgiving each other, just as in Christ God forgave you" (Ephesians 4:32 NIV).

CHAPTER 8
STRIVING: "FULFILL YOUR CALLING"

Many are the plans in a man's heart, but it is
the Lord's purpose that prevails.

—Proverbs 19:21 (NIV)

Sometimes it just feels like a typical day, and you're not even aware you are "striving"—that you're actually pushing yourself to your limit. That striving just starts to become a habit, an obsession.

Striving becomes part of who you are, just part of your personality. You keep telling yourself you are just "wired this way," that you were "born this way." The craziest part is, you totally forget about why you are consumed with pushing for more, why you want more, and why you believe running yourself into the ground is the only way to live and work.

We strive because

- we're disconnected from our true identity;
- our lives aren't aligned with our Lord;
- we measure our self-worth by worldly values; and
- we feel we can only gain acceptance and love based on our performance.

For a few years, a small chunk in time, I chased things built on a foundation of sand. I pursued fleeting things. In the end, they were things that ultimately didn't matter and could never truly satisfy me. I placed the world's version of success up on this pedestal, and when I crushed a goal, I set a new one and immediately asked, "What's next?" I wanted more, craved more. I was never satisfied. Looking back, my pursuit was all for selfish reasons. Ugh.

When I was in Jamaica with my husband, celebrating my fortieth birthday in 2017, all I could think about was my work and my new endeavor. I strove to meet the deadline I had set for myself as the launch approached, and I put it before anything and everyone else. It became this lofty goal on my priority list. I didn't even enjoy the blessings that surrounded me. I couldn't even conceptualize what "being in the moment" meant. Everything I have ever wanted was right in front of me. Everyone I loved with my whole heart stood before me. Yet I was distracted and couldn't focus. I was obsessed with achieving what I thought success meant in the world. I got caught up in a definition of success, which was hijacking my sense of self-worth. It stole so much from my family, and I know I will never get those moments back.

We often tell ourselves that our faith, family, friends, health, and career are our focus, usually in that order. But let's get real. How many of us just say that's what we value? Do we really *live* it? When it comes down to it, when we are faced with the everyday demands, the list ends up being a little more complex: career, laundry, cooking, cleaning, kids, family, you time. Faith ends up getting put on the back burner, and we revisit it when it's convenient or we have a free five minutes to even think or breathe.

Our faith gets relegated to the back burner of our lives; we know it's important, but it tends to languish until we "get to it." The relationship with our Savior, the relationship we need the most, gets ignored. The relationship that is always there for us becomes an afterthought. We categorize our faith amid all the chaos of our everyday lives. It too often falls off our radar of priorities when, in fact, it should be our primary focus. When we strive toward "the perfect life," we tell ourselves—with our long to-do lists, our unrealistic expectations of ourselves, and our long working hours toward the next career advancement; the dream home; the new car; the near-perfect, well-behaved kids; the task of being chauffeurs for our kids 24-7—that burning our candle at both ends is worth it for ourselves and our families.

We convince ourselves there is no other way to live, that a meaningful life has to come from strife. So we just keep on striving. We run on fumes, exhausted, pushing through on our own strength, telling ourselves we are living the "American dream," that constantly feeling overwhelmed with anxiety is the only way to get there. I'm here to tell you *it's a lie*. We keep trying to write and create our own story by taking control of the proverbial "pen." But I can tell you firsthand there is another way to live. I had no idea what I was missing out on.

- You mean, you can fold clothes and do dishes with a smile?
- You mean, you can advance in your career without always being stressed out and wracked with anxiety eighty hours a week?
- You can actually have fun with your kids?
- You can laugh and kick back?
- You can remember what it's like to "date" your husband?
- You mean, you can get everything you want out of life without missing out on all the things that mean the most?
- You mean, you don't need to perform to be loved?

One day while running on empty, I told Rob, "I hate the people I have become."

He looked at me with a blank stare and asked me, "How many of you are there?" We joke about it now and all the "people" I felt I was taking on, to my detriment.

Still, at my core, there was the "me" who wanted to drop everything and get on a path that felt 100 percent in tune with my heart and with God—to live and walk in faith, in authenticity, and in truth; to be completely aligned with who I was meant to simply *be*; to challenge what the world valued and honored with what I valued and gave my life purpose.

The other part of me was still stuck in what the world valued and held to be true. But I knew something felt off kilter, and it wasn't the life I wanted to live. I looked lovingly at my kids and realized instantly that I didn't want my kids to feel how I felt at that moment.

I didn't want them to ever feel the pressure to perform for love, to strive for perfection, or to believe their value and sense of self-worth were based on the world's superficial view of success. I wanted them to know that they were inherently loved, no matter what. That they are never alone. That life isn't about strife but about living a life destined to embrace *full faith* in the Lord, knowing He is our strength. That with Him all things are possible, since He is our peace. That He is always with us every step of the way and that His presence is a natural gift to us, not something we must strive for. But we should know intuitively in our hearts that it belongs to us without strife, performance, pain, or effort; but we should simply know that the love of God is our divine inheritance.

When we begin to seek Him and embark on that profound relationship with the One, it impacts our everyday life. When we live in the full light of God, it fuels us to show up as women who fundamentally have everything, and we gain exponentially in the peace that comes along with it.

I felt the full weight of what I was striving for in my life when things didn't align with who I truly was when I wasn't aligned with Him. God's sense of timing is impeccable, right? There is a sense of ease and harmony when you walk with who you truly are in alignment with Him, working on things that fill your soul, that build your soul, that define your soul, and that fall in line with the heart and will of the Lord.

Whether we stagnate, thrive, or fail, there is simply no comparison to alignment with God; it's a relationship with Him, not worldly achievement, that sustains us. In fact, worldly achievement is the ultimate trap. It's a trap I have fallen victim to and have been guilty of. I know how it can destroy true potential and prevent people from living their best, most authentic lives.

So let me begin by asking you this. What does success really mean to you? How do you picture it? What does it feel like? How do you define "success"? People usually fail because they don't take the time to define what they truly want; they are burdened by worldly standards that don't truly define who they are or what they are meant to do.

When we're confused, we attract confusion and chaos. We get distracted and feel lost, sad, left behind, depressed, unworthy of success, doomed, and destined to failure. But most of the time, we don't take the time to truly create our own definition of success.

So what would that look like for you? What's your definition? How would you develop your definition of success, which is genuinely built on your terms? Because I can tell you one thing: success isn't what others tell you it is. It is how *you define it for yourself.* If you believe success is what everyone else says it is, you're always going to miss the target.

And when you aim to achieve someone else's version of success, it's not going to mean as much to you; it won't have the same impact. I remember being caught up in this leadership advancement program in a company I was trying to advance in. The rankings, the titles, and the pressure were toxic for me and everyone around me. I felt like if I didn't advance, I was a failure. I remember crying in my closet quite often; looking back, I didn't know what I was thinking. I certainly chalk it up to a learning experience, but it sucked the life out of me. So I had to reevaluate my life and get back to whom and what I truly stood for. I had to define who I wanted to be and who I was meant to be. And that superficial version of success wasn't it.

It wasn't aligned with who I truly was. So I finally came to the realization that genuine success requires giving up other people's beliefs about what success really is. Forget about what other people think about what success means, what it looks like, what it requires. We've got to

82

stop comparing ourselves to those superficial definitions. Some people believe *success* is defined as being wealthy—having fame, fortune, or material wealth; being "lean, mean and strong"; and possessing the car, the house, the perfect family. The reality is that real success comes from within you; it's never anything material or external, and it's always driven from within you, on your own terms. So by understanding and valuing who you are and why you desire success, it's easier to tap into your true worth by becoming more aware of your strengths, skills, and God-given gifts.

Without getting caught up in the world's expectations for my clients, we talk about what a successful fitness and wellness journey looks like for them. I ask them to define what success means to them and how they can access it. How do we define success? Access to that is twofold.

It is often limited by someone else's definition.

We feel inadequate when we haven't measured up to an external standard. In doing so, we rob ourselves of the opportunity to define and appreciate our own unique experiences, our own unique gifts, and how we can impact our lives and others toward the greater good. The meaning of success is different for each person. You may not fit into other people's definitions of success. Still, you can give yourself permission to be okay with that. Success is an individual concept, and here's the exciting part. You get to define and design your own success, which will become the blueprint for how you live your life. Developing your own blueprint for success also means you get to create success on your terms. Suppose you are anything like me and have wrestled with what success actually means. In that case, it's time to actually take control of that narrative and determine what it means for you.

Let's think about our relationships, health, parenting, careers, professional achievements, material possessions, and overall happiness. What is your relationship to these fundamental aspects of life? Do you feel like you're trapped? Let's take our relationships. What does a successful relationship look like to you? Instead of comparing your relationship to that of the couple next door, how do you value yours? How do you contribute toward a better life?

A successful relationship can be defined only by you and your spouse or partner. Think about parenting. Everyone thinks he or she knows how to handle that one, right? I chuckle when people tell me what it means to be a parent. How many times do we compare ourselves to the other moms out there or compare our kids to other kids? We ate ice cream from the tub at 9:15 p.m. last night after a late-night basketball game. It sounds like poor parenting, but it works for us.

A while back, I shared a story about how I had lost it one day with my kids. You could say I was "a hot mess." I always thought I was "super mom," but now I know I am. I am in my own way. And so are you. We all are. Sometimes we invest in this idea about what a successful parent looks like and what a family should look like built on external standards. But what if we just came to the realization that the love and commitment we give to our family is what matters most, especially when it comes to being a successful parent?

How we achieve that varies; there is no set rule. And you get to determine what that means to you and your family, your career, and your professional achievements. I'm willing to bet you've worked really hard to get to where you currently are, but maybe you don't see that achievement, or you think you should be further along than you are right now in life. Maybe you see the accomplishments of your friends and colleagues. Still, you feel like you're spinning your wheels, comparing apples to oranges, which is the actual problem, right?

Because you're comparing in the first place. But think of the magnitude of what you have already achieved. We often lose sight of our everyday accomplishments. Take the time to be grateful and celebrate your accomplishments, journey, and impact you make every day. Without question, gaining material things can be an enticing motivation for working hard, but if you are just "trying to keep up with the Joneses," ask yourself, "Why am I competing in the first place?" You should enjoy whatever you earn rather than wasting your time competing with others.

But it's important not to forget that you deserve to be happy as well. Is that even a factor for you? What about your sanity, your peace? And I get it. It's all subjective. What makes one person happy may be totally inadequate for the next person, but remember that your overall happiness is nonnegotiable for your success.

When determining whether you are successful, ask yourself whether you're happy because they're both intertwined. When I cried in my closet, chasing someone else's version of success, I knew something needed to change. And that was my perspective—what I ingested, what I read, whom I surrounded myself with, who influenced me, whom I listened to, what I believed success was. To be honest, when it came to faith, I knew I had to start working on my journey.

And so I totally revamped my life, and I got back to what mattered the most. When you're doing yourself more harm than good and get distracted from your journey, you know that achieving success isn't about fighting yourself or fighting an objective view of how success is defined. It is about becoming the best version of yourself according to *God's* standards.

It is time to redefine what success means for you. Whatever anyone else is doing shouldn't play a role in your sense of self-worth or what success really means for you. Instead of comparing your accomplishments to those of others, focus on finding the light of success in your life. So, to embrace your definition of success, you need to understand how you perceive yourself objectively. I know it's easy to combat who you think you are every single day. The only thing that matters is how you show up today. The only competition you really have is against yourself, the person you see when you look in the mirror every single day.

And I get it. Most of us look at others and think, *Man, I would be so much happier if I did what they're doing.* We see others losing that weight, rocking out the burpees, running that eight-minute mile, and looking lean and unstoppable. We feel we can't achieve. Our insecurity starts to show, and our self-confidence drops to a new low, where we can't even attempt to move forward.

Let me remind you – to quote Theodore Roosevelt, "Comparison is the thief of joy." What you need right now is your own definition of success and a plan that works for you. I know there is a fire burning inside you, but we cannot allow comparison to cause us to question our own self-worth and happiness. We can't fall into the illusion of other people's lives built on social media and try to make them our own.

This can feel suffocating, stagnating. It feels like you're looking at a giant billboard of what your life should look like. But you feel disconnected from your authentic self. We live in a world where anyone can share a perfect snapshot of his or her life, and we interpret that as a success of how we should live. But we know reality is much different. Most people live with uncertainty and some degree of chaos, like we all do, neatly trimmed with social media posts. So we need to hold ourselves to our own standards, not someone else's viral video, okay?

The truth is, you're never going to hear anyone bragging about his or her struggles. The people who seem to always have it all together are those who have definitely experienced failure. Success is never built in a vacuum of inexperience. Suppose you actually knew how often they failed and picked themselves back up. In that case, you'd probably realize we're all similar in our struggles and aspirations. We "walk the same walk," so to speak. So you should compare yourself only to the person you were yesterday.

So get rid of your blinders, the distractions, and own your future. Find something that gives you passion and a sense of purpose. You have just as much talent and drive as the next person. So don't deprive the world of the incredible person you already are by competing with anyone else. You are totally unique. Don't sell yourself short by trying to be anyone else. Be grateful for the gifts you've been given and live with a mission that will impact the world. Just work on improving yourself every single day.

To put it simply, you ought to define and redefine what success really means to you so you can stop comparing yourself to others, playing second best. Allow yourself to be who God truly wants you to be.

I want to share with you a fundamental, heartfelt truth. If we don't start practicing our beliefs toward what we want, we'll miss a life that stands before us in plain sight.

I'm sure that resonates with you. So amid dreams, goals, and taking action, how do we get everything we want out of life? Well, it starts with gratitude. And I know that's a tired concept that has become pretty trendy over the last few years. I see it on T-shirts, on signs, and in social media. I know it's a hot topic in the mainstream. It's everywhere—in books, magazines, and blogs. I believe we see things we're looking for. So maybe this fact has just become clear to me, for whatever reason.

But you know what? If I said that gratitude improves your mental health and productivity, that it makes you happier and more relaxed, that it cultivates deeper relationships or helps you sleep better, and that it improves self-esteem, eases stress and anxiety, and fosters contentment, would you begin to realize it can have a profound impact on your life?

Would you believe me? No. Let me put it this way. I know it's really challenging to think about what you think you lack with a total focus on what you *do*. It's important to focus on what you should be grateful for. You might be at a crossroads, where you realize you need to make changes in your life, but you don't know where to start. How can something as simple as expressing appreciation make such a difference to your state of mind? Imagine if we could daily focus on gratitude and the impact it would have on our lives.

Just give it some thought. Would you feel calm or at peace? Would you stop nagging your spouse? Would people naturally want to be around us? Gratitude gives us energy. Would our careers take off if we focused on tackling our fears?

Would we crush the goals we've set for ourselves because we can push forward when we extract ourselves from a negative, ungrateful mindset? Would our enthusiasm and fire for life skyrocket? I'm just throwing these ideas out there. Here's the thing with gratitude. It can help you make positive choices, take better care of yourself, and feel empowered and develop a positive outlook. Yeah, I know you can adopt this attitude toward life, and you might say, "Right, but I can't handle it."

Stick with me here. I get it. We're human. We're not hardwired to feel gratitude. It doesn't come naturally to us. It's often so much easier to grumble to ourselves and complain and think about all the areas in our lives where we experience pain or hardship.

We need to reject the false gospel of living our lives in victimhood. We need to call ourselves out on our misperceptions, whether it's worrying about money or fretting about whether our partners truly understand us. Kids, our daily commute, and the traffic on our way to work drive us nuts every day. Whatever the reason is, our human nature seems to focus on what's going wrong in our lives. We dwell on what we don't have, which leads to a sense of powerlessness in life. We feel we're not getting everything we want out of life or at least not enough. Often we are blinded by this negative perspective when we don't get what we want or everything we think we deserve, everything we dream about.

If we keep hitting roadblocks in life, it's easy to feel powerless. Most of us have felt that life has dealt us a raw deal, that it's unfair. We wonder, *Why is this happening to me? Is this really all there is to life?* I've had many conversations. It's astonishing how many people think it's easy for successful, positive people to be grateful because they have so much to be grateful for.

Life isn't about success, money, jobs, cars, houses, or anything else in the material world. These things are illusory and don't ultimately contribute to your quality of life. They might temporarily. Sure, maybe.

But gratitude isn't about success or material wealth. Gratitude actually has to come first. It's the intro and the foundation to getting everything you truly want out of life.

"I will give thanks to the Lord because of his righteousness; I will sing the praises of the name of the Lord Most High" (Psalm 7:17 NIV).

Wake-Up Call Moments

We improve every day when we focus on our achievements and on what's good in our lives, along with all the blessings surrounding us. It's like we project the message: look at everything good we can have, which just produces more amazing things to show up in our lives. It's like the cycle of gratitude only builds on itself and just gets better. God has given us so much. If we just take the time to acknowledge what we owe Him in service to Him, we will feel profound gratitude for every gift in our lives, what we have now and what is yet to come.

That's exactly what we need to realize, even though we might not know it in distinct moments in our lives, with people entering and exiting our lives while we face our daily challenges. And when we extend this gratitude toward every aspect of our lives, we realize nothing is an accident in both good times and bad. Everything we experience is an opportunity for us to grow closer to God and become a grateful person who will utilize God's gifts. Some of us complain about and overlook all the blessings God has given us. The more we make use of His gifts, the more we will have. Does that make sense?

I could never finish counting all the things I owe God, and the more we practice gratitude, the more we see how much there is to be grateful for.

Your life then becomes this ongoing celebration, full of joy. You can create for yourself a life that has everything you truly want, and it costs you nothing. I encourage you to keep a gratitude journal. I started keeping one a few years back. It's important to become more aware of your surroundings. Begin to appreciate the little things, like a smile from a stranger, the smell of coffee brewing, or the sound of rain hitting your bedroom window. It's not hard to do. We just need to notice the good stuff in our lives.

I want to point out that intention with gratitude isn't about creating long lists that don't have meaning or value. I just don't want you to throw anything in your journal. I want you to express yourself and challenge yourself.

Think your way out of this. Articulate any painful experiences you've had, experiences you might be in denial about. It's important to express any upcoming failures you're dreading. Here the aim is to direct and shift your focus and live in a state of abundance. The next step is to differentiate "contentment" from "settling." Have you ever heard the saying "Be content but never satisfied"? I bring this up because I questioned this myself at one point in life. If you're content, does that mean you've settled? And if you've settled, does that mean you're content? Not necessarily. I've seen these terms used interchangeably, but I've started to realize that there's a massive difference between the two.

When you're content, when you're at peace with your faith, your life, your possessions, the choices you've made, you've lived up to your potential in life. But "settling" to me means selling yourself short and not appreciating what you should be grateful for, living a life of comfort but not fulfillment. But you always know you could do more. Are you settling for the life you have because it's easier to blame other people or the circumstances of your situation?

It takes work to discover what you should be grateful for in life. When we don't appreciate what we have, it's hard to feel content about our lives. So we settle. But we don't want to feel satisfied by just getting by. I want you to think about your talents.

What idols do you have in your life? What are you putting before and above the Lord?

Are you too comfortable living your day to day without focusing on your relationship with God? How is the Lord asking you to step out in faith?

How is He stretching you? What is He asking you to do that you're afraid of or feel that you're not equipped for?

Are you living your life and doing the work He has called you to do? If not, how does that make you feel?

It's okay to feel a desire to get more out of life, to pursue the next big thing. I want you to find true happiness. To me that means getting everything you want out of life. If you've settled and feel unfulfilled, it's time to make that change. I want you to revisit your goals and the vision you have for yourself of who you want to be. If your life or job doesn't support your goals or your vision, begin thinking about how you can make changes for the better.

Strife is a strong word, but when you strive for something, strive for contentment; and if you find yourself settling for a life or job you hate, it's time to change it. I can't stress that enough. Embrace the journey with gratitude for the blessings you have. We need to embrace this journey we call life.

I've learned to breathe, relax, and release all the worry and fear that pop up. When you relax and breathe, you open the door for more positive and prosperous things to come into your life.

So take that deep breath, relax, and focus on one task at a time. Remind yourself to stay present. Calm yourself down and go with the flow. This is what we all need to hear and practice.

Focus on what you're doing at the moment by mentally verbalizing what you're doing. I know that sounds so silly; for example, if you're washing your face, say to yourself, "I'm washing my face." That will bring you back into the moment. You can also do things more slowly. To do this, it's important to manage your time. So if you need to, get up a little earlier so you can practice slowing down a little. I know you'll benefit from getting up just a little earlier in the morning. You'll find it rewarding being able to live in the present and savor every moment because it's a true gift.

Go with the flow, take action, and pursue your dreams and goals, but then stop worrying and go with the flow.

The reality is that things don't always happen the way you want them to.

Sometimes things actually work out better than you planned, but you've got to go with the flow and make the best of every situation. When you go with the flow, you're not giving up on your goals or dreams. You're simply trusting in the bigger picture.

So I encourage you to relax and surrender because what you're seeking is also seeking you.

How can you live your life for God right now?

How is the Lord leading you? Are you allowing Him to guide your next steps and to strip the striving and idols from your life?

What does success look like to God? What does it look like to you? Do those visions align? Do you need to bend your vision to God's vision?

How does that differ from the world's view of success?

When we stop striving and come into a path of alignment, God is with us. We actually live out our purpose for Him instead of pushing ourselves in the wrong direction. We need to allow Him to lead us so we can fulfill our calling.

"Therefore if you have any encouragement from being united with Christ, if any comfort from his love, if any common sharing in the Spirit, if any tenderness and compassion, then make my joy complete by being like-minded, having the same love, being one in Spirit and of one mind. Do nothing out of selfish ambition or vain conceit. Rather, in humility value others above yourselves, not looking to your own interests but each of you to the interests of the others" (Philippians 2:1–4 NIV).

CHAPTER 9
THE POWER OF PRAYER

Pray continually, give thanks in all circumstances;
for this is God's will for you in Christ Jesus.

—1 Thessalonians 5:17–18 (NIV)

I honestly had no idea about the power of prayer, but I liked the concept.

But to be honest, I didn't have a clue about the authority we have and the magnitude of God's love and support for us. All I knew was that there had to be more for all of us. I never wanted to settle and lead a mediocre life in the sense that I didn't ever want to fall short of my true potential. I didn't want to leave anything unfinished and look back with regret. I wanted to lead a full life with every opportunity to live a life where that fierce faith fueled me to show up in a big way where God could use me as His vessel.

Yet I knew a piece of the puzzle was missing. I just felt a fire in my gut that there had to be more. I wanted my marriage to thrive. I wanted my kids to soar. I wanted doors to miraculously open, and I wanted my career to skyrocket. I wanted that peace, that unconditional love, that place of rest. I wanted that contentment. I wanted my first thoughts to come from a place of love rather than from bitterness, hurt, fear, or anger. I wanted to emanate joy with a healed heart. I wanted those encounters with God. I wanted not only to hear but also to listen to what God had to say to me. I wanted Him to guide my next steps and download the right words for me to speak with a clear perspective. I wanted Him to talk to me.

Why couldn't I hear Him?

My wish list was long. As my dad always told me, I had "wantinitis." I did. I wanted it all. Do we miss out on encounters with God? We probably have opportunities to connect with God all the time. Still, we miss them because we are so wrapped up in ourselves, we totally underestimate His power, or we fail to reach out and call on Him. Whatever the case may be, I want all of us to have an encounter that wakes us up to the fact that He is there for us.

It's so easy to praise Him when things are firing on all cylinders and when everything is working out. But it's when we struggle, when we get gut punched, or when we're confused and in the darkness that we truly encounter God and reach a breakthrough. Those are the game-changing moments in our lives. But we need to take notice.

He was right there on the day my mom passed away, and he was right there beside me when I was trying to navigate life without her. He was right there when the plow truck knocked me down. When businesses failed, he was right there when endeavors flourished, when relationships crumbled, when I hit rock bottom and questioned everything. He was there for me then as He is for me now, and the same is true for you. It took me forty years to grasp that concept. If you get anything from this, embrace this.

The Lord doesn't force us to change. We need to choose Him of our own free will. We need to invite Him in to truly experience His power. We need to ask Him to be with us. We have to pray to create the change we want to experience in our lives. How many times do we fight for what we want using only our willpower and strength, forgetting or not realizing the power of prayer? He's always been right there, available to us, but we need to ask. We need to pray. We need to pray about everything and anything.

God explicitly tells us that as long as we genuinely call out and pray to Him, He will accomplish everything we ask for. Now, with that being said, He might not answer according to our expected timeline or in the way we hope, but His response is always according to what we need. The way we get there and the path He takes us on will likely not be the one we started or paved for ourselves. But thankfully what prayer ultimately does is that it changes us. It changes our hearts from within. Prayer changes how we perceive the world and others. Prayer allows us to finally hear Him speak to us. It drowns out the noise of the world and our own thoughts, lies, and deceptions.

Prayer is just a call away that provides so much clarity.

Prayer builds the connection we need with the Lord.

When that relationship is strong, we find that missing piece of the puzzle. We are complete and full of the power He has given us. You might just be granted that mile-long wish list you have. Your relationships can be restored, and opportunities will become available to you. You will live a life of joy rather than one of fear. Prayer gives you the healing and forgiveness you so desperately need.

Life is going to happen. Chaos will surround you. And the Lord doesn't promise that you will never hit challenges. But He does promise that He will be there with you through it all; He has only has your highest good at heart. You will come out on the other side stronger and forever changed. He promises to work on everything toward your greatest good.

This is why we should always be active in our prayer; we should never become complacent with what happens in our lives. We can draw that line in the sand, drop to our knees, raise our hands, and cry out to God, whatever prayer looks like for you. We have the authority to make our voices heard in what happens in our lives. Once we embrace a life of prayer, we know what we are up against and can define what we want. For anything that steals our sense of peace and joy—fear, anxiety, doubt, or broken relationships—prayer is the answer for whatever we face. I've become the "crazy lady" shouting from the rooftops that Jesus heals. I get it now. I know prayer is the answer.

When my son moved out, I was faced with two choices. I could believe my son's lie that he wanted nothing to do with our family while playing the tough guy and being independently stubborn. And the lie was that I was a horrible mother because of it. I could allow the enemy to cause a division in my marriage and let the anger, hurt, and bitterness take over. I could resist tooth and nail out of pride and control issues, or I could get down on my knees and pray for restoration, healing, forgiveness, peace, and clarity—not just for myself but for my son, my husband, and my entire family. I was at war with myself. Mama bear was losing control. I chose prayer.

A few years ago, I would have fought but not in a way that would have been pleasing to the Lord. I would have fought and lashed out from a place of resentment and anger, trying to prove that I was right. Fighting with prayer would have never crossed my mind, but thanks to my prayer warrior sisters, who have been so pivotal in my walk (you know who you are, ladies), I am forever grateful for that encounter with God. I didn't want the burden of regret. I wanted my son and family to be reunited. But I knew I would have to change to get everything I wanted, for things to be different, to live differently. I had to stop blaming and trying to control everything. I had to stop feeling sorry for myself and feeling trapped.

It was through prayer that I was finally able to hear what my God had to say. He was directing my steps, and He gave me the ability to see through His eyes, the words to speak, and the power to restore my family. Prayer solved everything I thought was broken. Prayer changes you. He turned it all into good and transformed my life.

If we realize what prayer can do, we would invest in it and make a space in our lives for it.

It would be as important as sleep, food, and rest. Unfortunately, we just don't ask for it and humble ourselves enough to receive the answers that can come only through prayer. I am challenging you today. I am holding you accountable. All we need to do is reach out with faith and ask Him to touch our lives and intercede. Miracles will happen.

God will answer most powerfully.

Prayer Leads to Freedom

I'm not the same person I was just a short twelve months ago. When God moves, and we say yes ... believe me, He moves fast. It can seem far from our expectations, but in God's eyes, He always acts toward our highest good. By putting my faith in God's way and getting out of my own way, I've changed forever. You can say that by letting God take control of my life, I've finally graduated in my mind, and my heart has been renewed. I want you to experience this journey of strengthened and solidified faith.

It's like the prison cell we've built around ourselves brick by brick over our lifetime gets torn down. We experience a breakthrough. Each brick represents anger and hurt, pain, bitterness, fear, betrayal, doubt, jealousy, resentment, lack of self-worth, and unresolved conflicts. All the strongholds start to come crumbling down. We get to choose that transformation. Light begins to pour in. We can breathe again. We are free.

We need to experience complete surrender, complete release of worry and fear, and give it all to Him, walking with true identity, not the world's manufactured version of who we should be. Because when we do the work it takes, we are set free. We don't need to worry anymore or stress over people who don't understand the true us.

You want more for your life? You've got it. Now is the time to grab the freedom that surrounds you. Strife doesn't have to be a way of life. We're not meant to live a life of conflict. We're not meant to fix everything. You just need to set yourself free by showing up in the world as "the real you." That freedom comes from the One who will satisfy everything you need, the One who will protect and complete you. He will take all those missing pieces and any emptiness in your life, and He will replace it all with Him.

We know the truth. We now understand the inexplicable peace we have been craving. We now have that sense of calm from within, and we never want to go back to that prison cell. And the astonishing part about all this is that it's about coming to the realization that it isn't about you and me. It's 100 percent all about Him. Living with freedom means living His word and walking with His purpose. We learn that He works through us. He chooses us to be the agents of change by serving Him and others. We are meant to pursue Him and only Him. All the likes and love from the world, all the accolades and success we strive for, all the idols we need put up on pedestals, and all the approval we seek don't compare to the well He fills up for us. He will heal, forgive, and release all the bitterness and anger from within. There will be no more distractions or doubt. He will transform our hearts so love pours out from us. We will be living for Him. We will wake up each day on a mission to please Him. That is the definition of spiritual freedom.

I heard a story once at a leadership event that I absolutely love. Have you heard about the circus elephant chained to the ground by a stake? Let me tell you about it. I felt as though I was this elephant in the story. This huge, powerful, strong, vibrant animal couldn't move because of this tiny chain staked in the ground. Even this fierce, strong, twenty-four-thousand-pound elephant couldn't break free from his chain. He just stayed there and couldn't move. He didn't realize he could be free if he wanted to be. He could break free at any moment. But instead, he was trapped from his past experiences and had been unable to break free ever since he was a baby. He was chained to the past hurt, heartache, failures, beliefs, and what he thought was possible. He allowed all the negative challenges and offenses to keep him bound in place.

We can be free if we choose to be. We can be free if we surrender and let go. We can be free when we forgive and ask for forgiveness. We can be free when we give it all to Him and lay it down at the foot of the cross. We can be free when we change our beliefs and listen to the truth. We can be free when we surround ourselves with prayer warriors. We can be free when we allow Him to lift all oppression and misery. We can be free when we say yes to the Lord.

His voice is the sound of freedom. His unconditional love is freedom. The peace He provides is freedom. It's like we become childlike—dancing carefree once again. We discover that little girl inside us and let her loose, ready to soar to new heights, ready to show up as that fierce warrior princess on fire for the Lord. We allow God to use us as His vessels, living out His purpose for us and the path we are meant to walk. We are totally free because we are awake and fully embrace that God is always available and accessible to us if we just ask and surrender.

Wake-Up Call Moments

I want you to take a moment right now to close your eyes and focus on your breath and any tension you may be carrying. How do your shoulders feel? Are they up and around your ears? Are they relaxed? How about your jaw? Is it clenched? Can you take a deep breath without feeling anxious or lightheaded?

I want you to stretch out your legs. Reach your arms up high. Take a step forward and dance to your favorite worship song. Turn it up loud. Take another deep breath. Exhale.

I want you to experience freedom. True freedom.

After you've given it all to Him, I want you to return here and answer these questions to get more insight into where you are now and what's next in your walk with Him.

How has your heart transformed?

Can you recall a time where you allowed God to be in control because you trusted Him?

If you could remove one thing standing in your way from your calling right now, what would it be?

How is the Lord telling you to go and take action?

What chains do you need to break free from?

What will you have to do to be set free?

What does that freedom look or feel like?

Are you willing to hand it all over to God right now – the pain, the fear, the doubt, the past, all of it? Write your promise to God below. I promise to give you _____. I accept and receive your gifts of love and freedom.

Remember this: the Lord is our freedom. "Now the Lord is the Spirit, and where the Spirit of the Lord is, there is freedom" (2 Corinthians 3:17 NIV).

CHAPTER 10
FREE FALL

When you pass through the waters,
I will be with you;
and when you pass through the rivers,
they will not sweep over you.
When you walk through the fire,
you will not be burned;
the flames will not set you ablaze.
For I am the Lord your God,
the Holy One of Israel, your Savior;
I give Egypt for your ransom,
Cush and Seba in your stead.

—Isaiah 43:2–3 (NIV)

I'm sitting here, typing up this final chapter in the kitchen. The kids are coming in and out, worship music playing in the background, the boys constantly fixing food, the girls showing me their latest makeup look, the dryer buzzing. Interruptions galore, and let me tell you—our house is loud. Yet here I am, jumping into the mess and working through the chaos to give you a message. Here I sit with peace, calm, and complete trust, knowing this is exactly how it's supposed to be.

No more hiding in the closet, feeling alone physically, mentally, emotionally, and spiritually, because now I know the full power of the Lord Jesus Christ, and I'm here to tell you that my days of sobbing alone are gone. I assure you that you're not alone in that closet or on the floor or when you just feel like nobody else is there with you.

He is with you.

So I sit here, totally present in the chaos, jumping right in and enjoying the life right in front of me, ready to share with you what matters—the love of Jesus Christ.

Now, I must tell you that I never waved a magic wand. I didn't just decide to live a life for the Lord, and everything fell perfectly into place like a miracle. Life isn't perfect. In fact, even as Christians, we are met with so much adversity. Jesus tells us this. "I have told you these things, so that in me you may have peace. In this world you will have trouble. But take heart! I have overcome the world" (John 16:33 NIV).

Life isn't that easy. It takes commitment, bravery, trust, and the willingness to try something different. It takes courage to ask for help and to overcome pride, to know you can't fix everything and everyone on your own. But the first step is to let go and surrender.

When we decide to embark on the journey that strays from the mainstream, every day becomes a challenge. Let me be real with you for a moment. When you are on a mission to fulfill your purpose and live out the life God has planned for you, I guarantee you that there will be days when you just want to fall back into old habits and do what is comfortable. There will be times when doubt will creep back in, when you think you can't do it anymore, and the roadblocks will pop up out of nowhere just to distract you from your call. Constant roadblocks will start to feel like you are on this uphill battle that never ends.

You must press on and put yourself out there, the real you, standing strong in your belief ... and that can be every bit intimidating. People might resist you and pull away from you. Some people might plant a seed of doubt and insecurity within you, trying to keep you down. This is only because of the magnitude of your life's calling and the impact you will have on the lives of others. The enemy wants you to stay down.

If you're feeling attacked, remember this: "You must be important" (Pastor Steven Furtick).

The enemy will do all he can to stop the calling God has placed on your life. You may hear lies that you are unprepared and unworthy. But these are all lies.

Let me remind you—you have *everything* because of Him! You are fully equipped. Do not let anything stop you.

That missing piece of your heart, that missing puzzle piece, can be filled when you commit to doing the work.

But will we do it? Will we work on forgiveness? Will we work on healing? Will we work on the pain and old resentments? Will we work on surrendering completely? Will we open our hearts to our passions and calling? Will we invite Him in? Will we commit to a relationship with God?

We need to commit our lives to answer those questions with patience and grace.

Know that there is more for you beyond personal gain from one moment to the next. Christ isn't a quick fix but a lifelong commitment.

You may be asking Him, "What do you want me to do, Lord? What is next? What is my next step?"

The answer is right in front of you. But the real question is, will you embrace it?

Life won't always feel like complete bliss. It's work. It's a battle, trying to steer you off course, but it will all be worth it in the end.

There is no such thing as simply surrendering once. It involves several surrenders over time and deep spiritual reflection. It is a continual walk that requires the right support system and the right people in our lives, which leads me to what inspired me to do what I do now.

This feeling, this transformation, needed to be shared to help lift the fog. I was walking in your shoes just a short time ago.

I want everyone I know to experience this feeling. When you enter the unknown or come to a crossroads, I pray you will have the self-confidence in your potential to honor and follow that call on your life.

I said no for about four years straight. My friend invited me to go to a spiritual retreat every year. It wasn't affiliated with a specific church, just women gathering who wanted to praise the Lord all weekend. Honestly, it wasn't my kind of thing. I prefer to pray alone because my relationship with God is deeply personal. I didn't want people to see me pray.

But they knew I had a hunger and wanted to delve deeper with God, so they kept inviting me year after year. They wanted me to experience Him more fully. They told me the retreat was exactly what I needed, especially after all the chaos of 2020.

So I went.

I did something completely uncomfortable and out of my comfort zone so I could experience the purity of surrendering, the free fall into the arms of my maker.

I got to experience the comfort, the ease. No mask, no façade, just pure love … women who took me in, included me, and accepted me for who I was, no matter where I was in my walk. The most refreshing part was that they did that for everyone, and they'd do it for you too.

I close my eyes, and I'm moved to tears by the amount of love and energy I received there.

People prayed for hours, leaning in as they embraced complete surrender.

No agendas. No schedules. No expectations.

They were just led by the Holy Spirit.

I had never been a part of anything like that before, let alone to just be still for that long.

These women didn't hold back. I was told, "It will change you, it'll take over, and you'll be fundamentally changed after you leave."

They were right.

Thank goodness for friends who kept inviting me in, who were bold enough to share with me the secret to a life with Jesus, the healer of all things.

On that intense night, important words washed over me. They left their mark on me, and every now and then, I recall those words because I swear I could hear the Lord speaking through that woman praying over me. It felt like her words were straight from God's mouth to my ears. I took it all in.

She said that a pang of sadness over me was being lifted, that what I had gone through wasn't meaningless. I wrestled with the sadness and tried to rid myself of it. I eventually released myself from the sadness and grief, that place of darkness. I knew I would free myself of all of it with God as my backbone, as the voice that guided me in every moment.

He was going to fill and heal that void within me. He would turn my hardness into comfort, the hurt would turn into strength, the bitterness would turn into love, the resentment would turn into forgiveness, and the passion would turn into purpose.

You'll wake up just like I did.

The weight of my sadness left me. I knew my journey was all meant to prepare me for something, preparing me to launch into the world, taking up my mission, and answering the call He had placed in my life. This part goes back to my story, my fundamental message. I want to inspire women to be free through the grace, passion, and presence of the Lord.

So I led my own retreat in Sedona, and of course we worked on all the things we could let go of, what we could surrender to, and how we could take a leap of faith in our personal lives. The famous Slide Rock called our names. The water got pretty chilly as we approached it in late October. Yet that edge, that cliff, that leap of faith faced us at every moment. I chose to take a leap that day. Nothing stopped me, despite what others thought.

We jumped off the ten- to fifteen-foot red-rock ledge into the frigid water.

We totally submerged ourselves as the coldness took our breath away. It was like we were free, frozen, and falling into the unknown. Cold, wet, and shivering, we emerged out of the water, looking like smiling, drowned rats. The experience was fun. It felt exhilarating. It challenged us. It was the road less taken. It took us out of our comfort zones. It felt better than we would have imagined, and it was exactly what we needed at that time in our lives.

I encourage you to embrace your call and just own it. I challenge you to do the work it takes to answer that call and go through the discomfort and doubt it takes.

Now, I'm not telling you to plunge from a cliff into frigid water, but I am telling you that when you answer the call to follow Christ, the reward for the risk will be worth *all* of it.

"In the beginning was the Word, and the Word was with God, and the Word was God" (John 1:1 NIV).

Wake-Up Call Moments

In life we need to hike up the hill; we need to be the water carriers to refresh other people. When you refresh others, you will also be refreshed. "A generous person will prosper; whoever refreshes others will be refreshed" (Proverbs 11:25 NIV).

What you have gone through won't be wasted; the power of God won't be ignored.

We are called to be set apart by giving of ourselves and serving others, but we need to do the work on ourselves spiritually to be difference makers.

It's so important to take personal responsibility and look inward so we can answer the call.

How has your perspective changed? How are you seeing and hearing things differently?

How is the Lord working in your life?

How is your heart shifting as you step out into faith and hand the wheel to God?

How has focusing more on your relationship with the Lord changed your life?

Has anything tried to derail you – circumstances or people (maybe even yourself)?

What did you do to overcome these new challenges as you worked to build your faith?

How do you feel when freely submerged in God's perfect love?

How will you move forward in your life while putting God at the center?

"Being confident of this, that he who began a good work in you will carry it on to completion until the day of Christ Jesus" (Philippians 1:6 NIV).

CHAPTER 11
FINAL WORDS

Life is short.

I know we've all said that, but I want to tell you with deep conviction that it *really* is true.

In the blink of an eye, all your moments are adding up, creating a beautiful life, and it is preparing you for eternity.

The heart of it is that we get only one shot. We will cross the finish line at some point, and it'll be here before we know it. So I want to encourage you to truly live each and every day for Him. I encourage you to live fully awake, fully present, and fully for the Lord.

We need a revival in our souls. We need to wake up. We need to be on fire for God. Every day He is chasing us down in pursuit of our hearts, but it's up to us to slow down, just breathe, and let Him catch us.

Here's the thing. I know He isn't done with you. You're just now getting started, my friend. Don't think for one second that it's too late for you because it's not. So no more hiding, okay? No more being trapped in a prison of lies and deceit. I know that even if you feel like something is missing, He will replace every part of it with His unconditional and perfect love.

You are amazing, and now that you've heard it, I need you to believe it. Most importantly, He needs you to believe in yourself, so the next time the devil comes knocking at your door, you know what to say and do to get him out of there.

Repeat after me: "The devil can't mess with me. I belong to the Lord."

"For he chose us in him before the creation of the world to be holy and blameless in his sight. In love he predestined us for adoption to sonship through Jesus Christ, in accordance with his pleasure and will" (Ephesians 1:4–5 NIV).

So I ask, how will you spend the time you have been given? What if you don't hold back anymore? What if you give your life back to God? Do you have any idea what He can do in your life when you allow Him to do His mighty work?

I tell you, you have a calling on your life from the Lord. Don't wait to do what He asks of you.

I want you to think about all the hurt, pain, love, and breakthrough experiences it took for you to get to this very moment—and do something that most never do. Embrace it. Gather all the amazing God encounters and your gifts, talents, and unlimited potential, which have been buried, and use it all for good. Take a look in the mirror. You are still here for His reason … on purpose, for a purpose. So unleash that warrior in your heart. Life has a way of stealing passion from people. Many of us fall into the trap of just surviving, aimlessly walking. Even though we are awake, we are not really awake. Not today. Not anymore. I want you to feel totally alive from here on out.

This message isn't about religion and routine. This is about your calling and the relationship you have with the Lord. He is full of miracles; you're one of them. Walk with Him, and you'll discover carefree living and true freedom. You can cast away and give Him your fear, stress, anxiety, pain. All of it.

No more torment and bitterness, no more striving, no more carrying all that weight on your shoulders. You can surrender right now and let go of it all. Choose a life of joy. Choose a life *awake*! You cannot imagine what He is preparing for you … all the big things in store for you … all the love He has for you.

You knew there could always be more to this life. Now you are ready.

And He is waiting.

"Now may the Lord of peace himself give you peace at all times and in every way. The Lord be with all of you" (2 Thessalonians 3:16 NIV).

ACKNOWLEDGMENTS

My deep gratefulness to my husband, Rob, who has always been there for me, cheering me on and always loving me unconditionally. Walking through life with you is a true blessing.

Thanks to my kids, whom I love with all my being and pray for every day. You light up our lives. You are a true gift from God, and I love the noise, laughter, and chaos you bring to our home.

Love to my parents, Stuart and Tracy, who have guided me and helped shape me into who I am today. My heart is full.

Hugs to my prayer warriors and best of friends: Darcey, Leisa, Kari, Chrystal, and Jodi. Love you.

Love to my Gram, my grandparents, my brother (for always keeping it real)—and love to my bonus family, my in-laws, Mike and Marilyn.

My appreciation and love to the hundreds of women who have trusted me to help them on their life journey. The Fit & Fierce gang and the Just Breathe sisterhood, you inspire me daily.